THE KEY TO
THE GREAT GATE

Borgo Press Books by FRANK J. MORLOCK

Castor and Pollux and Other Opera Libretti (Editor)
The Chevalier d'Éon and Other Short Farces (Editor)
Chuzzlewit
Congreve's Comedy of Manners
Crime and Punishment
Cyrano and Molière: Five Plays by or About Molière (Editor)
Doctor Scratch and Other Plays (Editor)
Falstaff (with Shakespeare, John Dennis, & William Kendrick)
Fathers and Sons
Herculaneum & Sardanapalus: Two Opera Libretti (Editor)
The Idiot
Isle of Slaves and Other Plays (Editor)
Jurgen
Justine
The Key to the Great Gate and Other Plays
The Londoners & The Green Carnation: Two Plays
Lord Jim
The Madwoman of Beresina & Other Napoleonic Plays (Editor)
Notes from the Underground
Oblomov
Old Creole Days
Outrageous Women: Lady Macbeth and Other Plays (Editor)
Peter and Alexis
The Princess Casamassima
A Raw Youth
Salammbô & Dido: Two Operas (Editor)
The Stendhal Hamlet Scenarios and Other Shakespearean Shorts from the French (Editor)
Two Voltairean Plays: The Triumvirate; Comedy at Ferney
Whitewashing Julia and Other Plays
The Widow's Husband; and, Porthos in Search of an Outfit: Two Dumasian Comedies (Editor)
A Yiddish Hamlet and Other Plays
Zeneida & The Follies of Love & The Cat Who Changed into a Woman: Two Plays (Editor)

THE KEY TO THE GREAT GATE

AND OTHER PLAYS

FRANK J. MORLOCK

THE BORGO PRESS
MMXIII

THE KEY TO THE GREAT GATE

Copyright © 1986, 1988, 2013 by Frank J. Morlock

FIRST EDITION

Published by Wildside Press LLC

www.wildsidebooks.com

DEDICATION

To Al Segal

CONTENTS

THE KEY TO THE GREAT GATE. 9
   CAST OF CHARACTERS 10
   ACT I, Scene 1 11
   ACT I, Scene 2 40
   ACT II, Scene 3 66
   ACT II, Scene 4 71

HEROES AND ROMANTICS OF OUR TIMES 93
   CAST OF CHARACTERS 94
   THE PLAY 95

LADY LIBERTY 147
   CAST OF CHARACTERS: 148
   THE PLAY 149

THE WRITING LESSON 207
   CAST OF CHARACTERS 208
   THE PLAY 209

   ABOUT THE AUTHOR 224

THE KEY TO THE GREAT GATE
ADAPTED FROM A NOVEL BY HINKO GOTTLIEB

CAST OF CHARACTERS

DOCTOR HANS ANTON STRAUSS, a prominent Viennese attorney

DOCTOR GOTTLIEB

RABBI BENJAMIN PORETZ

SERGEANT WEICHSELBRAUN

DOV TARNOPOLSKI

A GUARD

THE LIEUTENANT

ACT I
SCENE 1

Cell 84, the Vienna City Jail, on a Monday in 1942. There are three occupants of the cell. The cell is overcrowded. The occupants are Jews. Dr. Hans Anton Strauss, a prominent Viennese attorney who specialized in Criminal cases until the Anschluss, is playing chess with the Chief Rabbi of Salonika with improvised chessmen. Dr. Gottlieb, a Jew from Zagreb, is trying to write in a dirty notebook. He is paying no attention to the players. The players, however, take a great interest in their game, for the Rabbi and the lawyer are natural antagonists, and delight in beating each other by hook or by crook.

Strauss (gleefully)

Check, my dear Rabbi.

Rabbi (after a moment, triumphantly)

Checkmate, Dr. Strauss.

Strauss

Bah, you tricked me.

Rabbi

Serves you right, freethinker.

Strauss

Reactionary.

Rabbi

Godless turncoat.

Strauss

I keep telling you I am not Jewish, I'm a Catholic.

Rabbi

Tell that to the Nazis.

Strauss

I do, I do; they don't believe me.

Rabbi

So, why should I? Lie to them if you like.

Strauss

Look here, I'm not lying. My great-grandfather was Jewish, it's true, but the family has been Catholic since 1798, and I have baptismal certificates to prove it.

Rabbi

Forgeries. Some of your clients provided you with those certificates.

Strauss

I only defend bank robbers and businessmen.

Rabbi

Another game, councilor?

Strauss

This time I'm going to beat you.

Rabbi

Just be careful not to move the pieces when I'm not looking, if you please.

Strauss

You wait and see.

(The cell door is suddenly pushed open by Sgt. Weichselbraun, who looks a bit like Hitler. Weichselbraun is accompanied by a new prisoner, Dov Tarnopolski, who wears a long black coat and is extremely tall. The prisoners jump to attention.)

Weichselbraun

A new companion for you, straight from Poland.

Rabbi

This is incomprehensible—surely you don't mean to put him here?

Strauss

The cell is already overcrowded. This is inhumane treatment, and—

Gottlieb

We can't possibly fit a fourth man in here.

Weichselbraun

You'll just have to sleep on top of each other like rats.

(Weichselbraun thinks this remark is highly witty and laughs appreciatively.)

Tarnopolski

My name is Dov Tarnopolski.

Weichselbraun (going out)

Correction. You are prisoner number 434—and you're a piece of shit, like all Jews.

(Weichselbraun leaves, slamming the door behind him.)

Tarnopolski

I am Tarnopolski, Dov Tarnopolski.

Gottlieb

Hinko Gottlieb from Zagreb. Writer.

Rabbi

A free-thinker and atheist. I am Benjamin Poretz, from Salonika.

Strauss

A real reactionary, too. I'm Dr. Felix Strauss, a criminal lawyer before the war.

Rabbi

And a worse freethinker than Gottlieb, if that's possible. He pretends he's not a Jew. Are you a Jew, Tarnopolski?

Tarnopolski

Of course. Cigarettes?

(Tarnopolski hands out several cigarettes.)

Strauss

Impossible. They take them away from the prisoners.

Tarnopolski

Help yourselves.

(Tarnopolski now produces three packs and distributes them, to the astonishment of the others.)

Tarnopolski

What's the name of the son-of-a-bitch who brought me here?

Strauss

Shh! Be quiet, for God's sake. Someone might be listening.

Tarnopolski (yelling)

FUCK HIM!

(Dr. Strauss goes into a corner and cringes, mumbling something.)

Strauss

This is unheard of, unheard of.

Rabbi (after a pause)

We are being inhospitable. Will you have some food?

(The Rabbi displays some soup.)

Tarnopolski

No, no. I couldn't possibly eat that!

(Tarnopolski disdainfully turns away, then produces a big piece of French bread and some salami and starts eating.)

Gottlieb

He's got—food.

Rabbi

Real food.

Tarnopolski

Have some, I've got plenty more.

Strauss

They never let prisoners bring food into the cells.

Gottlieb

Eat, Dr. Strauss, eat. We'll explain the mystery later.

Tarnopolski (casually)

Want some cake—or maybe some strudel?

Gottlieb

Cake? I haven't seen cake since 1939!

Strauss

Strudel! Strudel!

(Tarnopolski produces some cake and strudel which he passes out.)

Rabbi

All right, so far. Is there anything more? No black coffee?

Tarnopolski

No, I haven't any coffee—but I can offer you some good coffee liqueur.

(Tarnopolski produces a bottle of liqueur and four little glasses.)

Strauss

Stop! Now, I know these are delusions.

Tarnopolski (shaking his head)

I can't do tricks like a fakir. Have a drink and convince yourselves.

Strauss

That's rich! As if you didn't know we are incapable of doing so—the way you have influenced our senses. Our senses fool us. They send false reports to our brains. How are we to control them? But, if someone had taken a motion picture of us—it would have been obvious that we're eating newspapers, not cake and strudel.

Tarnopolski

I haven't any movie camera. But, tell me, did you enjoy the strudel?

Strauss

Delicious! Absolutely delicious delusions.

Rabbi

Never had a better cake.

Gottlieb

The best Viennese cake I've ever tasted.

Tarnopolski

Then, you enjoyed it? What more do you want? Suppose it is pure Viennese tap water I offer you? What keeps you from drinking it?

(Tarnopolski drinks some liqueur.)

Strauss (timidly, closing his eyes, tasting his drink)

It goes down just like liqueur.

(The others also drink.)

Tarnopolski

What do you think of the bouquet? Grand, isn't it? And the color?

(Tarnopolski holds the bottle up to the light.)

Gottlieb

Heavenly.

(They all refill their glasses and drink again. "Prost! Cheers! Bottoms up!" They begin to sing, timidly at first, then drunkenly, as they gain in self-confidence. Suddenly Weichselbraun yanks open the door.)

Weichselbraun

What the hell is going on here?

Strauss (drunken and friendly)

Hallo there, Weichselbraun, friend of my youth—

Weichselbraun

Hands off—

Rabbi (stepping up)

Field Marshal Poretz, hic—

Weichselbraun

Well, look at that. The Jews are soused. (glaring at the liqueur bottle) Who brought you this liqueur?

(Weichselbraun glares all around and finally looks suspiciously at Tarnopolski. Tarnopolski remains defiantly seated and unmoved by Weichselbraun's rage.)

Strauss

That's not liqueur, Weichselbraun, it's suggestion.

Weichselbraun (puzzled)

What?

Strauss

Yes, suggestion! Haven't you ever heard of it? Suh-gez-shun! Not surprising you've never heard of it—you're fearfully ignorant.

Weichselbraun

Achtung!

Strauss (confidentially)

Don't be an ass, Weichselbraun. Try and understand. Hocus-pocus, and so on. Why do you say liqueur? Get a movie camera and you'll see. We've eaten a lot of bunk—but no cake. No cake, Weichselbraun. No cake.

Weichselbraun

Cake! Very soon I'll make you eat shit!

Strauss (hurt)

Why are you always so cross with me? Don't you think I notice it? Come here and kiss me, Weichselbraun.

Weichselbraun

Kiss you! Kiss my arse! Is this your kind of a joke? Who brought you the drinks?

Tarnopolski (easily)

No one. I had them with me.

Weichselbraun

Ach, so. So, you brought them with you. And Weichselbraun who searched you, when you were brought in, didn't notice anything, eh? Weichselbraun is a blind fool who doesn't know his job, eh? (hysterically) Is this some dirty Jewish plot to get me in trouble? You BASTARDS! Me, Weichselbraun, who has searched thousands of prisoners—just overlooked a liqueur bottle and four glasses?

Tarnopolski (calmly)

Six, as a matter of fact.

(Tarnopolski puts two more glasses on the table.)

Weichselbraun

What! What else do you have in your pockets?

Tarnopolski

Nothing, as you see.

(Weichselbraun frisks him again and turns out his pockets.)

Weichselbraun

Of course, they're empty. This is a plot. (goes to the Rabbi) Poretz, you're a Rabbi, so you shouldn't lie even if you are a Jew. Who brought you the drinks?

Rabbi (helplessly)

I, I—

Weichselbraun

All right, I see that you are lying, too. But, you're wrong if you think you can fool me. (working himself up) Who gave you that liqueur? (silence) You don't want to talk? You want to try me to the limit? Very well. You'll get your way, my dear Jews. You'll have your miracles. Just wait.

(Weichselbraun sweeps up everything on the table and starts carrying it out.)

Tarnopolski

Leave the matches. How do you want us to light our cigarettes?

Weichselbraun (menacingly)

What cigarettes?

(Tarnopolski holds out his hand with cigarettes in it. When Weichselbraun reaches for them, Tarnopolski closes his palm. After considerable effort Weichselbraun forces Tarnopolski's fist open. The cigarettes are gone. Weichselbraun is amazed and Tarnopolski is ironic.)

Strauss

You see. Hocus-pocus.

Weichselbraun

You wait—you'll see.

(Weichselbraun stares at Tarnopolski, then turns on his heel and rushes out.)

Tarnopolski

Well, now that that fool is gone, we'd better get some matches.

Strauss

Matches!

Tarnopolski

I've got plenty of cigarettes for everybody, but we'll need matches.

Rabbi

But, that is impossible, we saw him search you.

Tarnopolski

Let's see if we can get the guard's attention. (at the door) Hey, open up!

(Tarnopolski pulls out more cigarettes and distributes them.)

Guard (thundering)

Silence!

Tarnopolski (politely)

Do you have any matches? Weichselbraun confiscated ours, now we can't light our cigarettes.

Guard

You fellows really have cigarettes?

Tarnopolski (offering some)

Here.

Guard

Thanks, but I only smoke cigars.

Tarnopolski

What do you say to some Havanas?

Guard

I love them. But they haven't been seen here in a long time.

Tarnopolski (pulling out a box)

Help yourself.

Guard

Thank you, very much. Here are some matches. I'll bring some more tomorrow. Have you ever been to Mistelbach?

Tarnopolski

No. Never heard of the place. I'm from Poland.

Guard

I'm from Mistelbach—and that's why I'm a little nervous about this transaction.

Strauss

You, a member of the master race, afraid?

Guard

Mistelbach is not far from Vienna. Some years ago, before I was born, a magician came to our town. He gave a performance in the town hall. At midnight, after the magician had performed many devilish tricks—suddenly from all sides, water started pouring into the hall. The ladies had to pull up their skirts. What a show! But, then the water suddenly disappeared, and the magician was gone. So was the mayor's silver watch and chain. Now, what do you think? Won't I get a piece of hot iron in my hands if I take one of your cigars?

Tarnopolski

Don't be afraid. I'd give you the whole box, but Weichselbraun would give you trouble if he saw you with it.

Guard

All right, I'll trust you. Now, excuse me, there's something I have to do. ALL RIGHT, YOU DAMN JEWS, GET BACK IN YOUR CELL AND DON'T RAISE ANYMORE RUCKUS OR I'LL BEAT YOU ALL TO A PULP. That should make Weichselbraun happy. (goes out)

Strauss

That guard is not a bad sort. He never abuses us, except for the record.

Gottlieb

What will the poor idiot think when he searches his pocket for your cigar and doesn't find it?

Tarnopolski

Why shouldn't he find it? I've already told you that I'm not a magician.

Gottlieb

You underestimate me. You can confuse my senses—but you have no power over my mind.

Tarnopolski

You're talking nonsense, Gottlieb. How can you separate your mind from your senses? But, let that go—

Strauss

The man says he's not a magician, what does he take us for?

Gottlieb

Neither was Merlin, nor Simon Magus.

Tarnopolski

What do you know about the theory of relativity?

Gottlieb

A Jew named Einstein invented it—otherwise, it's all Greek to me.

Strauss

What has the theory of relativity got to do with your illusions?

Tarnopolski

They are not illusions.

Strauss

Forget you're on stage, Tarnopolski, and tell us how you do it.

Tarnopolski

They are not illusions.

Rabbi

Perhaps, they are miracles.

Strauss

And Tarnopolski is the Messiah.

Tarnopolski

They are not miracles.

Gottlieb

But you are the Messiah, eh?

Strauss

Stop playing games with us, please. Have fun with Weichselbraun if you like, but be honest with us.

Tarnopolski (somewhat annoyed)

I am not playing games. I cannot perform magical tricks. But, I can, within certain limits, make things smaller or larger. Smaller or larger in relation to other things.

Gottlieb

Aha! You've invented a hydraulic press that reduces bottles and cigars to a hundredth of their former size. Is that it?

Tarnopolski

No, not quite that. No pressure is involved. But, it is true that I can make a reduction in a certain system of things.

Strauss

In other words, you have discovered a process whereby you can reduce our earth to the size of an apple. A fine thing to do!

Tarnopolski

My power does not go so far. The earth is enclosed in its cosmic system and I cannot change that. All I can do—

Gottlieb

Ah, now I have it. You took your cigars out of your cosmic system. That's what you wanted to say, isn't it?

Tarnopolski

I see that I shall have an easy time making myself clear to you. You have more knowledge than I anticipated. You understand quickly and correctly.

Strauss

Hocus pocus. Hocus pocus. You'll get us all killed. How could you be so irresponsible as to just stand there with that cigarette in your mouth? What will Weichselbraun think of us, especially of you?

Tarnopolski (maliciously)

Of me? Why should Weichselbraun get a bad impression of me?

Strauss

Don't you realize the seriousness of our situation?

Tarnopolski

Have no concern on my account. Weichselbraun saw you, not me, with a cigarette in your mouth. Just a little hocus pocus, you understand.

Strauss

This is an unbearable impersonation. I shall enlighten Weichselbraun.

Tarnopolski

Try it, by all means. But you won't meet with success. It will sound to Weichselbraun as if you were swearing your head off at him. Hocus pocus again, you understand?

(Strauss goes off in a corner and fumes. Tarnopolski produces a gigantic salami and offers some to Gottlieb, who, despite his astonishment, takes a huge piece. The Rabbi declines.)

Rabbi

Thank you, but I can't.

Strauss

I don't understand you, Rabbi. I can't make out your point of view.

Rabbi

It's not kosher. That's my point of view.

Strauss

I understand refusing the prison meat, I myself am a pious Catholic. (the others laugh) I respect another man's religious conviction. I fast on Good Friday. But, in the kind of reality we're living in now, your ritualistic food laws cannot apply.

Rabbi

And, why is that?

Strauss

Because, just as you could dream of eating ham and eggs without sinning, surely you can take this imaginary salami without committing a sin.

Rabbi

You talk like a lawyer—but you forget that religious laws are not like laws in your sense of the term.

Strauss

I dispute that.

Rabbi

You dispute everything. In your courts, you judge actions which are against the law, and where there is no evidence there is no guilt!

Strauss

What's wrong with that?

Rabbi

But, in the realm of religious laws, no importance is attached to evidence. I can eat meat ten times a day and not commit a sin if I don't know I am eating meat and the ignorance is not my fault.

Strauss

A nice legalistic distinction.

Rabbi (triumphantly)

But, I commit sin even when I eat kosher if I suspect that it is not.

Tarnopolski

I'm sorry I don't have kosher salami. But, if you insist on eating kosher, then prepare your own food.

(Tarnopolski produces a live chicken and hands it to the Rabbi, who stares in astonishment.)

Gottlieb

The man has supernatural powers!

Rabbi

A miracle.

Gottlieb

That's what I mean.

Strauss (still the skeptic)

Suggestion—mere suggestion.

Gottlieb

Nonsense.

Tarnopolski

Please, gentlemen, I am a scientist, not a miracle worker.

Strauss

Scientist! He's a veritable Paracelsus!

Tarnopolski

Certainly. Dov Tarnopolski at your service. Fellow of the Polish Academy, a correspondent and disciple of Einstein.

Strauss

What in the name of God have your illusions to do with Einstein?

Tarnopolski

Relativity. You see, we know so very little about space. You cannot help it. Man's power of imagination is limited. We think of space as sort of an empty container which we can fill up.

Gottlieb

And I think so, too.

Tarnopolski

It is now possible to say that space is matter without mass.

Gottlieb

So?

Tarnopolski

On the basis of this knowledge—

(Weichselbraun enters with the Guard.)

Weichselbraun

Achtung, Juden!

(They all freeze except Tarnopolski.)

Weichselbraun

Tarnopolski!

Tarnopolski

What is it?

Weichselbraun

Who brought you the bottle?

Tarnopolski

Listen, Weichselbraun, you are getting on my nerves with your questioning. Even if I were to tell you how the bottle got here, you are much too stupid to understand. You're behaving like a jackass, and you haven't any manners, either. You haven't even so much as wished us a good day. Make sure you don't omit that next time. Do you understand? Now, you may go. Hurry, because your face makes me sick.

Strauss (rushing up)

Do you recognize me, Weichselbraun? My name is Strauss. Look at me carefully.

Weichselbraun

What the devil do you want?

Strauss

Look at me carefully. This is I, I, personally. That one over there only seems to you to be Dr. Strauss, but he is Tarnopolski. Don't believe a word he says.

Weichselbraun

Have you gone crazy? What do you want?

Strauss (agitated)

I am Dr. Hans Anton Strauss, criminal lawyer. I have handled over seven thousand cases before the courts of this city before the Anschluss. I can produce numerous witnesses to attest to my identity. If you doubt me, ask the Rabbi, or Gottlieb. But, that one over there is Dov Tarnopolski. Don't let him put one over on you, Weichselbraun!

Weichselbraun

They've gone mad. (to the guard) Take these three outside. (pointing to Tarnopolski, the Rabbi, and Strauss)

Guard (pointing his weapon)

Kommt!

(The three go out with the Guard.)

Weichselbraun

There, that's better. Now, you—you've always been a reasonable man, perhaps you will be reasonable now. I've always treated you well, haven't I?

(Gottlieb remains silent.)

Weichselbraun (irritated by the silence)

You make no complaint, do you?

Gottlieb

No. No complaint.

Weichselbraun

Gut. Who brought you the drinks? (silence) Who brought you the drinks?

Gottlieb

Tarnopolski admitted that he brought it. I really don't know more than that.

Weichselbraun (getting nasty)

So, you don't know more than that! And he brought this bottle along in his pocket, did he?

Gottlieb

That's right, he pulled it out of his coat pocket.

Weichselbraun

Well, that's just what I wanted to hear. Put the bottle into your pocket. (he gives the bottle to Gottlieb) Why do you look at me so stupidly? Into your pocket, I said.

Gottlieb (trying unsuccessfully)

It doesn't fit.

Weichselbraun

Well, what a surprise! Now, tell me, where did you get the liqueur? Did Kurz bring it?

Gottlieb

No. Kurz didn't bring anything except aspirin for Dr. Strauss.

Weichselbraun

It had to be Kurz. Nobody else could have brought it into the cell. Confess!

Gottlieb

It wasn't Kurz. Just watch Tarnopolski.

Weichselbraun

Why should I ask that liar? So! You don't want to confess? You don't want to!

Gottlieb

Tarnopolski will explain it all. He knows all kinds of magic tricks—it's got something to do with relativity and Einstein.

Weichselbraun

Who's Einstein? Look, Jew, don't trifle with me. If it wasn't Kurz, it must have been Knoll.

Gottlieb

No. Knoll didn't bring us anything. Why don't you ask Tarnopolski?

Weichselbraun (in a sadistic rage)

You don't want to talk, you don't want to talk. I'll teach you to talk.

(Weichselbraun lashes Gottlieb in a fury of impotent rage.)

BLACKOUT

ACT I
SCENE 2

When the lights go up, all the prisoners are back in the cell.

Tarnopolski

Let me have a look at your arm.

Gottlieb

It's nothing.

Tarnopolski

Why didn't you tell me about this immediately?

Gottlieb

Let it go. It's all over.

Tarnopolski

You should have told me.

Strauss

What I hate about this place is that you can never get any news.

I'd pay twenty marks just to be able to listen to London.

Tarnopolski

How much?

Strauss (cagily)

Ten marks.

Tarnopolski

Give me ten marks and you shall listen to London.

Strauss

The money is here.

Tarnopolski

Voilà!

(Tarnopolski displays a radio. The cord seems to end in his pocket.)

Strauss

Another one of your illusions.

Radio

"German motorized divisions suffered heavy losses between Smolensk and Warsaw."

(The prisoners all huddle around the radio.)

Radio

"Sixteen German submarines were sunk this month."

Prisoners

Hurrah!

Rabbi

It's amazing.

Strauss (frightened)

Someone is listening at the door.

Radio

"Hitler is wrong if he thinks he can break the resistance of the democratic freedom-loving peoples. His present success may well fool the Germans—"

(Weichselbraun appears.)

Weichselbraun

But, what is this?

Tarnopolski

A radio, Weichselbraun. Listen, you haven't heard anything like it in years. Sit down and enjoy yourself.

Radio

"—but Hitler, that criminal, and all his evil followers will not escape the punishment they deserve. Churchill has said—"

Weichselbraun

This is—do you know that this is? You'll be brought to court for this. Stop or I'll shoot. Stop, I say.

(Weichselbraun brandishes his Luger.)

Tarnopolski

Don't get excited, Weichselbraun. You don't have to tremble for your beloved leader. Listen, now comes the best part.

Weichselbraun

Listen! I'll get the Lieutenant and let him handle this nest of subversives.

(Weichselbraun goes out. Tarnopolski turns off the radio.)

Strauss

I congratulate you, Tarnopolski. Now you've really got us into something. Three days ago I read in the paper about a janitor who was condemned to death for listening to enemy broadcasts.

Tarnopolski

How could I know that? I'm a stranger here. And besides, it was you who ordered the radio. You're the intellectual originator, and you alone bear the responsibility. You will be shot, Hans Anton. It's a pity you were baptized, we won't be able to come to your funeral.

Strauss

Don't crack jokes. I insist you get rid of the corpus delicti instantly.

Rabbi

I think it would be advisable.

Gottlieb

Dr. Strauss is right.

Tarnopolski

All right, I'll do this favor for you. But on one condition. Turn around and cover your eyes.

Strauss

This is ridiculous.

Rabbi

We are not schoolchildren.

Tarnopolski

I insist.

Strauss

Very well.

(The other prisoners turn around and cover their eyes.)

Tarnopolski

No cheating, please, Dr. Strauss.

Rabbi

Say when.

(There is a sudden, short blackout. Suddenly we hear the sound of Liszt's Second Hungarian Rhapsody on a piano. As the lights go up, we see Tarnopolski seated on a stool playing at a piano that wasn't there before. The Lieutenant and Weichselbraun enter.)

Lieutenant

Weichselbraun, I always knew you were stupid, but even you should be able to tell the difference between a radio and a piano.

Weichselbraun

I don't understand this, sir. When I saw it, it was small. And it didn't play, it talked.

Lieutenant

Hmmm! I well believe you are incapable of understanding this. But, these Jews cannot fool a German officer. Not me. You know what this is? A hoax. A very ordinary, very cheap, Jewish hoax.

Weichselbraun

Yes sir. A cheap hoax, as the lieutenant says, sir.

Lieutenant

It's done with springs and buttons.

Weichselbraun

Springs and buttons.

Lieutenant

Press one spring, a radio. Press again, a piano. Do you understand me now, Weichselbraun?

Weichselbraun

Yes, sir.

Lieutenant

You have only to find the spring.

(Tarnopolski has been playing throughout this conversation and continues to play as the Lieutenant fumbles around for the button.)

Lieutenant

Now, where is it? Patience, Weichselbraun.

Weichselbraun

Patience, sir.

Lieutenant (crawling under the piano)

A little patience and I will find the button.

(The Guard comes to the door.)

Guard

Herr Lieutenant, you have an important telephone call.

Lieutenant (irritated)

Who is it? I'm busy.

Guard

Berlin, sir.

Lieutenant (scrambling to his feet and hitting his head on the piano)

Heil, Hitler! (rushing out) Come, Weichselbraun. We'll attend to this later.

(Tarnopolski plays a final flourish and slams the piano like a professional concert pianist as Weichselbraun follows the Lieutenant out.)

Rabbi

What will we do when they come back?

Tarnopolski

I have another surprise for them.

Strauss

Enough of your surprises. Your surprises are going to get us all killed.

Tarnopolski

That's what they mean to do to us anyway, is it not?

Strauss

That is not entirely certain. With proper behavior, it may be possible to appeal to their moral sentiments, and they will have no excuse—

Gottlieb

They need no excuse.

Strauss

They are not totally uncivilized. We will draft an appeal to the highest authorities protesting—

Rabbi

To Hitler, perhaps? A fine idea.

Gottlieb

Perhaps, you will finish your explanation of how you do this.

Tarnopolski

Just what kind of explanation are you talking about?

Gottlieb

Tarnopolski doesn't merely know how to pull pianos out of his pocket; he has a scientific explanation of how it is done.

Rabbi

Theories! Theories! The hungry infant yells for the breast and a nurse puts a rubber nipple in his mouth. Man is hungry for enlightenment and the scholar feeds him theories!

Tarnopolski

I'm not a scholar. There's no substitute for enlightenment. A theory is just a mirror. We control observations through observations, experience through experience, and theories through theories. Man cannot find his way out of such a circle.

Rabbi

Very good! Now, you have reached the point where I wanted you. Your overbearing agnosticism doesn't help you out of it.

Tarnopolski

What makes you think I want to get out of it? I am a tourist. Satisfaction lies in the voyage itself.

Rabbi

Only vagabonds and thieves travel without destination.

Tarnopolski

Is this, in your opinion, a natural or a moral maxim? I'm too weak a partner to be able to discuss moral laws with you.

Rabbi

I do not accept this distinction. Moral and natural laws have the same origin.

Tarnopolski

What moral laws? I know several.

Rabbi

I know only one.

Tarnopolski

The Dalai Lama in Tibet says the same thing—so does Hitler. In five thousand years all moral laws have undergone changes.

Rabbi

That is emphatically not true.

Strauss

I suggest this interesting discussion be postponed. I hear them coming.

Tarnopolski

Gentlemen, if you will turn your backs again.

(The others turn away. There is a quick blackout and when the lights go up the piano is gone. The Lieutenant and Weichselbraun enter.)

Weichselbraun

My wife had a table you could pull out.

Lieutenant

That is something entirely different. A piano is not a table you can pull out.

Weichselbraun (flabbergasted)

It's gone!

Lieutenant

It's clear. They have pushed it in and put it away. We'll find it in a minute.

(The Lieutenant begins peeping here and there, gets down on his hands and knees, but soon becomes frustrated. Weichselbraun, in spite of himself, is amused by the absurdity of his superior.)

Lieutenant (noticing Weichselbraun)

What makes you grin, Sergeant? (yelling at Strauss) Watch out, or I'll smash in your ugly snout! (pause, titters) Which one of you is Tarnopolski?

Tarnopolski (coolly)

I am.

Lieutenant

Where have you put the piano?

Tarnopolski

Have you seen a piano here? I don't know anything about it.

Lieutenant

Don't act up, Jew. I'm asking you officially—where is the piano?

Tarnopolski (with studied insolence)

My dear Lieutenant, you're making a mistake. It must have seemed that you saw it. Do you often have such illusions?

Lieutenant (hysterically)

Give me the piano, immediately, do you hear? Immediately!

Strauss (terrified)

Give it to him.

Lieutenant

Do you understand what I am telling you? I want the piano! Where have you hidden the piano? Give me that piano! Where is it? Talk! (jumping up and down) Give me the piano! I've seen it, it must be here! Do you hear? Give it here. I want that piano.

(Slowly Tarnopolski removes a tiny piano from his pocket and hands it to the Lieutenant, who stares at it, stupefied. Then he fumbles with it.)

Lieutenant

Where is the button? Uh, you swine. Do you make fun of a German officer? You will see. Just you wait.

(The Lieutenant exits in a tearful fury followed by Weichselbraun.)

Strauss

What will happen now? Tarnopolski, don't you have any sense of what you are doing?

Rabbi

He's right. If you wish to play ducks and drakes with your own life, so be it. But, we prefer to live a bit longer.

Gottlieb

I still would like to know how he did it.

Tarnopolski (displaying a small object)

Gentlemen, my pocket condenser.

Strauss

Listen, Tarnopolski—with your apparatus you could—

Tarnopolski

Certainly, I could.

Rabbi

What good would that do us? We're on the third floor.

Tarnopolski

That would make no difference to me! If I wanted to escape, I could get out through the keyhole and take you along with me.

Strauss (enthusiastically)

Let's go!

Tarnopolski (with a sweeping gesture)

I haven't come to this prison just to get a few Jews whom I don't know out of it.

Rabbi

Then, you won't do it?

Tarnopolski

It's possible that I will do this favor for you—if I'm in the mood. But, it's just as possible that I won't.

Gottlieb

Your cavalier attitude is outrageous. You will not exercise your power to assist innocent people in the utmost distress—unless you are in the mood.

Tarnopolski

The three of you apparently think that I will turn my good thousand dollar bill into small change to give away to beggars penny by penny. Has it ever occurred to you that I have the key in my pocket that opens the gates to all the prisons in the world?

Gottlieb

No, it had not occurred to us, but if that is the case—if there's more to you than mere vaudeville, why—?

Rabbi

And you? Has it occurred to you, that you, with this key in your pocket, are just as much responsible for our imprisonment as Weichselbraun and Hitler if you refuse to help us.

Tarnopolski (complacently)

Of course, I have thought about it.

Rabbi

And, what do you say to it?

Tarnopolski

For the moment, nothing.

Strauss (turning around and walking to his corner in a fury)

Nothing! Nothing!

Tarnopolski

Let me show you something else. Do you know anything about acceleration?

Gottlieb

Acceleration?

Tarnopolski

The smallest object accelerated to a certain intensity acquires enormous energy.

Gottlieb

So?

(Tarnopolski takes off his shoe and throws it to the floor. There is a loud explosion. A siren suddenly goes off.)

Guard's voice

That was a bomb.

Strauss (coming out of his corner)

Look. There's a big hole in the floor.

(Enter Weichselbraun and the Lieutenant.)

Weichselbraun

What happened here? Tarnopolski, what is this hole?

Gottlieb

We don't know ourselves. Suddenly, there was a crash and then this hole.

Weichselbraun

Shut up! (to Tarnopolski) You are being asked. Stand at attention! (kicking Tarnopolski)

Tarnopolski

You can see for yourself. Just a hole. But, I want to show you something else. (pulling Gottlieb over and exposing his arm) Do you see this, Weichselbraun? Why did you torture this man,

Weichselbraun? I want to know why you beat a defenseless man?

(Weichselbraun looks puzzled at first, then hits Tarnopolski a tremendous blow in the face.)

Weichselbraun

So! Now you know.

Tarnopolski (getting up and wiping away some blood)

Of course, now I know.

Lieutenant

Did it stink of sulfur in here?

Strauss

It stinks of carbolic acid and—

Weichselbraun

But, who threw the bomb?

Lieutenant

Who else but the English?

Weichselbraun

We have no reports of the English over Vienna tonight.

Lieutenant (wisely)

You can't know about it if they're flying in the stratosphere.

Weichselbraun

Nonsense!

Lieutenant (icily)

Pardon me? What did you say?

Weichselbraun (standing his ground)

That is nonsense, I said. How can a bomb get through a windowpane without breaking it?

Lieutenant

Ah, I see, the windowpane. That is, of course, an argument. The windows were of course, unhooked and let down. You should occasionally inspect the cells at night, Weichselbraun.

Weichselbraun

Maybe the windows were let down, but (brightly) there is the matter of the bars.

Lieutenant

Right, the bars. But, you will admit that a bomb could squeeze through them?

Weichselbraun

If it isn't too big.

Lieutenant

It wasn't. That you can see for yourself.

Weichselbraun

And the English threw it horizontally through the bars from the plane?

Lieutenant

Not exactly horizontally, but in an extended parabola. (cagily) You know, of course, what a parabola is, Weichselbraun?

Weichselbraun

A parabola?

Lieutenant

A parabola, little Weichselbraun.

Weichselbraun

No. I'm not curious. I know what I know. The parabola is a fraud.

Lieutenant

How dare you say that to me, Weichselbraun?

Weichselbraun

All right, in a parabola. But, please, the bomb comes flying horizontally through the window into the cell—and crashes vertically to the floor. I don't know. I only ask: how this can be?

Lieutenant

That, of course, I am asking myself, too. There's only one answer for it—the bomb brushed against the bars in passing through.

Weichselbraun

But, the bomb would have exploded.

Lieutenant

If it didn't fail. It was probably a time bomb. The English throw bombs like that.

Weichselbraun

I think the Jews had a hand in it.

Lieutenant

All right, all right, Weichselbraun. We know this song of yours already.

Weichselbraun

This is not a song, you wait and see.

(The Lieutenant and Weichselbraun go out.)

Tarnopolski

I am sorry you don't like my food, Rabbi. But, if you would like to visit me at home, I'm sure we could find something to eat there.

Rabbi

When does the next train leave for Poland?

Tarnopolski

Who's talking about Poland? My house is here. Like a snail, I carry it with me, except it's in my pocket, not on my back.

(Tarnopolski produces a small house and puts it on the table.)

Strauss (impressed)

We didn't know you had a house.

Tarnopolski

Didn't I tell you that? I must have forgotten. It's not actually my house, if belongs to a friend of mine.

Rabbi

But, how are we going to get in there?

Tarnopolski

You'll see.

(Weichselbraun returns.)

Weichselbraun

Tarnopolski, take all your things and follow me.

Tarnopolski

Where are you taking me?

Weichselbraun

You'll find out.

Tarnopolski

And my shoes? I have no others, and these slippers aren't mine.

Weichselbraun

I don't give a damn about your shoes. Whoever has taken them away from you can give them back. Are you ready? Forward, march.

Tarnopolski

I can't go without my shoes.

Weichselbraun

Why not?

Tarnopolski

I'm not used to walking around in my bare feet. I might catch cold.

Weichselbraun

You aren't going? You aren't going, you say?

Tarnopolski

I said, I cannot go without my shoes.

Weichselbraun

I'm warning you, Tarnopolski. We know how to handle malcontents like you.

Strauss

You'd better go. Resistance is useless.

Tarnopolski

Without my shoes, not another step!

(Weichselbraun turns on his heel and walks out.)

Strauss

This was unnecessary.

Rabbi

You are not bringing danger only to yourself, but to us, too!

Tarnopolski

What, in your opinion, will happen now?

Gottlieb

Nothing special. You don't have to be afraid. A little squad of SS will come to pay us a visit. A very little squad. No more than ten men. They will knock gently at the door and gently and politely ask you if they can come in. If you're busy at the moment, they're accustomed to waiting. You have no idea how polite, civil, and kindly they are.

Tarnopolski

Then, I don't have to make any preparations for my defense?

Strauss

Not in the least. Absolutely not. It happened twice that down on the first floor the SS fired a volley into a cell and a prisoner was killed. Two others seriously wounded. Friendly misunderstanding.

(A sound of clanking feet comes down the corridor and stops in front of the cell door.)

Weichselbraun (from outside)

Load!

(All the prisoners except Tarnopolski dive for cover.)

BLACKOUT

As the lights go up, Tarnopolski has produced a large antiaircraft weapon aimed straight at the door.

Tarnopolski

Fire.

Weichselbraun (as he opens the door)

What the—

(A tremendous flash and explosion. Silence.)

Tarnopolski

Nobody will disturb us anymore tonight, gentlemen. Come, supper is waiting.

(The others slowly get up and stare as the curtain falls.)

CURTAIN

ACT II
SCENE 3

When the lights go up, we are in the library of a large European Villa. Tarnopolski is leading in his three guests. The library is in some disorder.

Tarnopolski

You don't have to be afraid. We are now entering the area of concentrated space. You must excuse all this. Some German soldiers lived here for three days. Before that it looked much friendlier, you may be sure.

Strauss

Where exactly was this place?

Tarnopolski

This villa was in a Polish village less than twelve miles from Warsaw.

Rabbi

What happened?

Tarnopolski

A very famous architect used to live here with his two daughters.

Gottlieb

It's quite a place.

Tarnopolski

I was invited to stay here before the war broke out. The main part of my work was finished at that time. I set up my laboratory in the cellar. The architect was the only person who knew about my research. It was amazing, the Germans left us alone for the longest time. One day, I went to buy some material in a nearby town, and when I returned German soldiers were in the house.

Rabbi

What about the architect and his daughters?

Tarnopolski

Gone! Vanished. They'd been taken away before I could find out where or by whom. My questions made the soldiers suspicious. I was brought before their Lieutenant, who was a young boy, no more than eighteen. When he found out I was a Jew he ordered me shot.

Gottlieb

Ah, Germans.

Tarnopolski

He was such a nice-looking boy, too. Well, they picked on the wrong Jew. I used my condenser and shrank them to the size of toy soldiers, and I kicked them out of the house.

Strauss

But, why did you shrink the house?

Tarnopolski

Because it was dear to me. Besides, if the Germans had come back, who knows what they would have done to it?

Rabbi

But, what about the owner and his daughters?

Tarnopolski

I could get no definite information. Several signs pointed to the fact that my friends had been taken to Vienna. That was the reason that I came here.

Strauss

And it was here you were arrested by the Gestapo.

Tarnopolski

That's right.

Strauss

On what charge?

Tarnopolski

No charge has been made.

Gottlieb (looking at a woman's picture)

Was this your friend's wife?

Tarnopolski

Yes. She died the year the picture was painted. She was driving her car and collided with a bus. She died instantly. A beautiful death.

Strauss

Why do you say that?

Tarnopolski

Dying instantly is better than dying old and burned out inside.

Rabbi

The Germans have other plans for us.

Strauss (who has been busying himself at the table)

Dinner is served, gentlemen.

Rabbi (with a champagne glass)

To your health, Tarnopolski.

(Tarnopolski takes a large champagne glass from a shelf.)

Rabbi

Are you going to serve us champagne?

Tarnopolski

Unfortunately, no. I need the glass for other purposes. Enjoy your dinner, gentlemen. I am going away for a little while. Don't worry if I'm gone a little longer than that. You are perfectly safe here. Nothing can happen to you.

(Tarnopolski goes out.)

BLACKOUT

ACT II
SCENE 4

When the lights go up, the three prisoners are all tense.

Rabbi

Where is he?

Gottlieb

He said we shouldn't worry.

Strauss

Why should we not worry? I'm worried.

Rabbi

Where is Tarnopolski?

Strauss

He's coming right back.

Gottlieb

He's been gone several hours.

Rabbi

I don't hear anything—and it's terribly dark outside.

Strauss (pouring a drink)

Let's state the case.

Rabbi

Stop it, Strauss.

Strauss (louder)

Let's state the case! What if something has happened to Tarnopolski?

Rabbi

Nonsense! What could have happened to him?

Strauss

How should I know? All right—only academically. I know that Tarnopolski will come back. With his powers he can suffer no harm. I don't doubt that at all! Only, I'm asking myself, what do we do if he doesn't come back?

Gottlieb

We'll be all right.

Strauss

Our cell is blocked in some way so the Germans can't get in. Very well. Our house is standing on the table in the cell. So, good. We are in the house and safe. Even better. But what I want to know is, if Tarnopolski does not come back, can we leave this house at all?

Rabbi

You have talked over Tarnopolski's theories with him. You seem to understand it better than we do. What do you think?

Gottlieb

I'm sure he'll come back.

Rabbi

Will we be able to get out if he doesn't?

Gottlieb

Maybe, but I doubt it. His laboratory is in the cellar. Perhaps, with time, I could fathom his notes, if he left any lying around.

Strauss

It's bad enough to die like a rat. If you're a Jew, you get used to that idea, but to die the size of a rat—

Rabbi

So, you admit you are Jewish!

Strauss

I admit no such thing. I was merely expressing my horror of the situation.

Rabbi

Bah!

Gottlieb

I rather wish we were back in Cell 84.

Rabbi

Do you know what freedom is?

Gottlieb

Yes, I think I know.

Rabbi

No, you don't know. And I don't know either. If I knew, I wouldn't be homesick for Cell 84. I wouldn't be homesick for Weichselbraun and the comfort of a dirty overcrowded little cell. How do we get back into it?

Gottlieb

I have no idea.

(Enter Tarnopolski.)

Strauss

Are we glad to see you!

Tarnopolski

Sorry, I'm a little late.

Strauss

I've never been so glad to see anyone in my life.

Rabbi

The blessings of the Lord are many.

Tarnopolski

Sit down, I've brought you something.

(Tarnopolski holds up the champagne glass. In it is the miniature figure of Weichselbraun.)

Strauss

Look at that!

Gottlieb

He can't get out.

Tarnopolski

He'll never beat anyone again. This is the end of Weichselbraun.

Strauss

Why didn't you resist him when he hit you before?

Tarnopolski

If I had followed my first impulse, I would have killed him.

Rabbi

That would have been just, but not advisable, in view of the danger.

Tarnopolski

I could have done it without any danger.

Gottlieb

How?

Tarnopolski

Nobody would know that I had killed him. He would simply have disappeared, dematerialized down to the last nail in the heel of his shoe, and his disappearance would have remained inexplicable and mysterious.

Rabbi

If I were you, I would have killed him.

Tarnopolski

I'm glad I didn't listen to the voice of my primeval ancestors. I've never killed a man, never even thought I would. But, if I had killed Weichselbraun, how would I be any better than he?

Rabbi (indignantly)

And you think you have to be better than the Germans? Better than the German who killed your brother, robbed your father, and raped your sister? Who humiliated you, spat at you, and mistreated you? Should we answer the concentration camps with kindergartens?

Tarnopolski

Are you under the impression I have answered Weichselbraun with sedatives? I have said, I repeat it, I don't want to be a murderer.

Rabbi

So forget all about it? Forgive them?

Tarnopolski

Just because I want to be better than Weichselbraun doesn't mean I want to pardon criminals or fraternize with them.

Rabbi

You're talking like a textbook on ethics. An eye for an eye and a tooth for a tooth. That is the law. You growled at me before because I hoped that you would help us escape. Do you think it would be an irrational use of power to help a man who has been thrown into prison unjustly?

Tarnopolski

I shall have to disappoint you. Yes. That, too, would be an irrational use of power.

Strauss

Then, you won't help us!

Tarnopolski

I may help you—but you are only three among millions who have suffered a similar fate. Why do you think you have earned preferment above all the others?

Strauss

Helping us in no ways prevents you from helping others.

Tarnopolski

I can't go from cell to cell and let you out the back door one by one. My key opens the great gate.

Rabbi

Your philosophy is confused. You don't want to pay out petty cash or to spend your capital. We have heard everything you don't want. What do you want?

Tarnopolski

I have difficulty answering that question.

Rabbi

Why? It's a simple question.

Tarnopolski

You would have no trouble answering such a question because you have clearly defined limits.

Rabbi

And how are you any different?

Tarnopolski

My case is different. My possibilities are infinite. My case is unique without precedent. Besides, I have never been greedy for power. My only passions, other than mathematics, are good music and a good cigarette.

Rabbi

In your place, I would—

Tarnopolski (interrupting)

It doesn't matter what you would do in my place. I alone am faced with the decision, and what I do must agree with my ideas of the world and not yours. Who wants more coffee?

Rabbi

I will make some. I learned the business in Greece.

Tarnopolski

Weichselbraun disturbs me here. (he puts the glass in the cupboard) In this room, I definitely established the scientific basis of my condenser. I'm sorry I can't give you a complete picture of the work I've done, what false leads I had to overcome. I really can't say how I had the patience to start over again so many times.

Rabbi

The dreamer does not give in!

Tarnopolski

My architect friend is intuitive while I am analytical. So, I consider my first task is to find him and get his advice. And I certainly will not undertake anything else before I've found him.

Strauss

We understand that, but you haven't found him since you got here, or done anything in the way of looking for your friend.

Tarnopolski

That isn't entirely correct. When I went to get Weichselbraun, I first went to the reception office and took a look at the files.

Rabbi

And?

Tarnopolski

I didn't find the architect, but I ascertained that at about the right time a shipment of prisoners was brought to Vienna from Warsaw.

Strauss

It isn't impossible that the architect is still in Vienna. The Gestapo keeps certain prisoners in its own custody.

Tarnopolski

Have you any idea where?

Strauss

Probably in the building that was formerly the Hotel Metropol on Moritz Platz.

Tarnopolski

Is that far away? I don't know much about Vienna.

Strauss

No, it's not far. You can't miss the building, it's huge.

Tarnopolski

How about the cells? Where are they?

Strauss

I'm not sure, but I suspect in the basement.

Tarnopolski

I might still go there tonight. If I don't find the architect here, I fear I'll have to go back to Poland.

Rabbi

If I had been you, I wouldn't have come here at all without reliable information.

Strauss

Hunting like this only loses valuable time.

Tarnopolski

If the architect can't be found here, then, of course, I've made a mistake. But he was a quiet, withdrawn person who did not stand out in either wealth or politics—so I suppose the Germans would treat him no differently than the other three hundred thousand Jewish intellectuals who were arrested at the same time.

Strauss

But, was he known in professional circles?

Tarnopolski

He was known. Two years ago he received first prize in an international contest to redesign the state opera in Rio de Janeiro.

Strauss

Therefore, he was an exceptional person. We must assume the Germans knew about him.

Tarnopolski

But, why would they separate him from the others?

Strauss

We cannot be sure. Maybe he seemed suspicious because of his connections abroad.

Gottlieb

Possibly they needed him to serve in their war machine.

Tarnopolski

He would never have lent himself to that.

Strauss

Certainly. But, if he refused to cooperate, you may be sure they treated him accordingly.

Tarnopolski

Damn them!

Strauss

These are idle speculations. You must look for such persons as can give you positive clues. With your condenser that is no problem whatsoever.

Tarnopolski

What should I do, in your opinion?

Strauss

Return to Poland and try to find a trace of him right there. The farther you go from there, the smaller your chances are. You will have to proceed quickly, energetically, and unscrupulously.

Tarnopolski

Unscrupulously!

Strauss

Certainly—when needed. And it will be needed. You are dealing with the Gestapo.

Tarnopolski

You are right. In the morning I shall go back to Poland. Can I count on your help?

Strauss

We shall help you. Leave the organization of the search to me. I have experience in such matters.

Rabbi (swatting at something)

A moth.

Strauss

Leave it alone. Why do you want to kill it?

Rabbi

Why should I spare a destructive animal?

Strauss

Because this destructive creature is an important factor in the mechanics of capitalist society.

Rabbi

But, last summer, your important factor ate up my coat and my wife's furs.

Strauss

Yes, and millions of dollars' worth of dinner jackets, overcoats, scarves, oriental rugs, draperies, and blankets.

Rabbi

All the more reason to destroy such a destructive creature.

Strauss

Nonsense. Think how many sheep ranchers, weavers, textile factories, seamstresses, not to mention merchants, this poor moth keeps busy. This little moth in the last analysis also supplies part of your income as Rabbi.

Rabbi

You don't say so! I was under the impression that I depended on my kehillah. I must immediately inform my wife of this.

Strauss

It's one of the paradoxes of our way of life. We could not possibly remove the negative elements which destroy human products without stopping the wheels of industry and putting millions out of work.

Rabbi

So! The moth is not harmful. No doubt you will propose to raise them and put them under legal protection.

Strauss

That's not a bad idea, Rabbi.

Rabbi

Perhaps you would be satisfied to found an international institute to investigate means of improving their living conditions.

Strauss

That's an even better idea. If I do, I will name it after you—the Moritz Institute.

Rabbi

Do you by chance have another scheme which would allow us to exterminate moths?

Strauss

Of course I have.

Gottlieb

Strauss has a scheme for everything, depend upon it.

Tarnopolski

It seems to me we are not meeting here to resolve this question, however interesting. The Rabbi asked me, what do I really want? After listening to this, I think I can answer you now.

Rabbi

Hear, hear!

Tarnopolski

When I finished my research, I felt overjoyed with a feeling of accomplishment and power.

Rabbi

Natural enough.

Strauss

Certainly, yours is a stupendous achievement.

Tarnopolski

To live means to resist the threats of nature. When man found he could resist better by joining with other men, he created the social contract. Thus far, everything is clear and simple.

Rabbi

Clear and simple blasphemy.

Tarnopolski

I need society, society needs me.

Strauss

This is good. I could use this argument with a jury.

Tarnopolski

In other words, I am social and I am disposed to use my power socially.

Rabbi

Hear, hear!

Tarnopolski

There are four of us in our cell. We have common desires and troubles—in this respect our interests are identical. But, we each have individual interests in conflict with the common interests. In short, we are a little society.

Strauss

Ah, but we are here against our will.

Tarnopolski

Whoever decides for himself what society he will be a member of? We are born into society and few of us ever change.

Strauss

That's true, that's true.

Tarnopolski

On the other hand, everything that we consider social is not necessarily social for Cell 83 next door.

Rabbi

So, what do you deduce?

Tarnopolski

From this, we deduce that every society, in pursuing its common goals, runs into the danger of coming into conflict with other societies which have an equal right to exist.

Gottlieb

None of this is new.

Tarnopolski

Certainly not. I am not a social innovator. But, you see, I, more than any other man, possess the power to overcome nature. I could become a tyrant over the rest of mankind. But, that would not be enough to assure me of my fundamental right.

Strauss

What right is that?

Tarnopolski

Happiness. For the most part, I cannot change the conditions of nature. I doubt whether I would render humanity a service by doing so.

Rabbi

I agree with you. If man always had what he needed he would be, without knowing it, infinitely happy—but then he wouldn't be able to read or write.

Tarnopolski

Man does nothing that he doesn't have to do.

Rabbi

So, you conclude what, exactly?

Tarnopolski

Man is happy only when searching for a better life.

Rabbi

But, man lives in the present.

Tarnopolski

If I could be sure that any one order of society would make men happy I would force it on him, because it is within my power. But there is no such order.

Strauss

There you are right. There is no law that will make man happy.

Rabbi

There is God's law. Living is happiness enough if we do not distort the meaning.

Tarnopolski

Leave man to himself and he will find his own way. (excitedly) Man is governed through his imagination. Because of an invisible god and an invisible paradise, he'll let himself be driven by emperors, popes, demagogues, and dictators.

Rabbi

There you go again with your freethinking. You make sense one minute, then you start your blasphemy.

Tarnopolski

Technical progress now makes it possible to do without such substitutes. A machine gun is cheaper and easier to handle than a bishop.

Strauss (maliciously)

Or a rabbi.

Tarnopolski

But, machine guns are conquered by other machine guns—and above them all, stands Dov Tarnopolski, the unknown Jew from Warsaw.

Strauss

What are you getting at?

Tarnopolski

It should be enough for people to hear about me. It should be enough for them to know that somewhere in the world there is a man who fears no man, whom no one can subjugate or kill. A man whose arm reaches through the most powerful armor into the darkest hiding places. A man who wants neither recognition nor honors. A man who wants neither to command nor to be commanded. There is only one thing I will not tolerate. Selfish power, violence, or tyranny! That is what I want.

Rabbi

Twenty-five centuries ago, Lao Tze said that the wise man operates without action, creates without effort, does good, and vanishes.

Tarnopolski

And vanishes.

(Suddenly, he and all the characters vanish. There is a silence. The stage remains empty and the curtain falls.)

CURTAIN

HEROES AND ROMANTICS OF OUR TIMES
A COMEDY IN ONE ACT, ADAPTED FROM A PLAY BY HENRI DUVERNOIS

CAST OF CHARACTERS

Dobbs, a police Corporal

Dillon, a police officer

Larry Chambers, a police Sergeant, about thirty years old

Jack Dalton, the Sheriff, about thirty-five years old

Mitch Powell, an unemployed waiter

Vonda, about twenty-five years old

THE PLAY

The scene takes place in the office of the Sheriff in Atkinsville, a mid-sized American town somewhere in the heartland of middle America.

The stage is empty when the curtain rises. We are in the office of Sheriff Jack Dalton. On the walls are posters for missing persons and criminals and duty rosters. The office contains a desk, several chairs, and a rather fancy couch. After a moment Corporal Dobbs and Dillon pass through. It is late at night.

Dobbs

Sheriff Dalton must still be at the theatre.

Dillon

He surely likes to see the plays. Never cared for that much myself. Too highbrow. I like the movies.

Dobbs

I think the Sheriff likes one of the actresses.

Dillon

Now, don't you be spreadin' scandal.

Dobbs

I ain't spreadin' no scandal. You put up with too much shit from him.

Dillon

What're you talkin' about?

Dobbs

You like to kiss his ass.

Dillon

You're just runnin' your mouth again.

Dobbs

You know what I'm talkin' about. You should stand up to him more.

Dillon

Leave me alone, Dobbs.

(Enter Sergeant Chambers.)

Dobbs

Evening, Sergeant.

Chambers

Hadn't you boys better get back on patrol?

Dobbs (fawningly)

We was just on our way, Sarge. Things been quiet though.

Dillon (to Dobbs, on their way out)

Why don't you stand up to him more?

(Exit Dobbs and Dillon. They greet Sheriff Jack Dalton, who comes in jauntily and tosses his hat on his desk.)

Dalton

Evening, Larry.

Chambers

Evening, sir. Did you like the play?

Dalton

Oh, it was almost too hot to enjoy it. Rotten weather. Anything new?

Chambers

Nothing, sir.

Dalton

You sure?

Chambers

Oh, the reporters came for information.

Dalton

Over the Tucker business? (Chambers nods) I hope you were nice to them.

Chambers

Disgustingly nice, Sheriff.

Dalton

And that's all?

Chambers

Some drunks, as usual, on a Friday night. A couple of brawls, a couple of thefts, and that's that. Nobody hurt.

Dalton

That's good.

Chambers

Nothing happening in Atkinsville. Never is, for that matter.

Dalton

Wonderful. Maybe I'll be reelected.

Chambers

At the moment, Atkinsville is reposing in perfect tranquility.

Dalton

Superficial tranquility, Sergeant. There are volcanoes grumbling in their depths. Nobody came to ask for me?

Chambers

Nobody. Was it a success?

Dalton

What?

Chambers

The new play.

Dalton

Huh! Big house—very big house. Some pretty women—lots of them. Same as always.

Chambers

Ah, the theatre.

Dalton

Bah, very deceiving, the theatre.. Most plays drag, tiring, repetitious situations, banalities—never raise any social problems. Shit.

Chambers

Hell, we deal with social problems here, Sheriff, on a daily basis.

Dalton

We're married to them, you could say. All you see on the stage is love affairs. "Take me, I'm yours." Adultery, whatever you wish. Reform, ideas never—

Chambers

The theatre doesn't think.

Dalton

No, it's a fact. It's because the theatre caters to women. God, that's the reason—no need for further explanation.

Chambers

Right.

Dalton

Almost midnight. You know, I don't need you on a quiet night like this. Go on home. Take off. I've some work.

Chambers

That's very kind of you, sir. (hesitating) Sir, by the way, have you heard anything about my article?

Dalton

Your article? Right, I forgot. I saw the publisher of the *Sentinel* the other day—

Chambers

Well, uh?

Dalton

Well, it seems it won't do. Too heavy, your article. Too heavy. What they want is something light—witty.

Chambers

But it's a serious study of crime based on actual cases in our files.

Dalton

What can I say? I told them that. It's not my idea.

Chambers (very disappointed)

Thanks all the same, Jack. And people complain about the press! Decadence.

Dalton

Everything's decadent, Larry, the press, the theatre, the public, the police, too. Especially big city police—not here in good ol' Atkinsville, population thirty thousand,. We live in an epoch of decadence. What do you want? We're not going to be born again, you know. Good night.

Chambers

It's all the same to me. But it's sad—very sad. (dejected) Good night, sir.

(Sergeant Chambers goes out. The Sheriff works, whistles, looks at the clock impatiently, as if he is waiting for something to happen.)

Dalton

Should be here by now. (working some more) Any time now. (works some more) C'mon, dammit.

(Noise of a scuffle outside, a woman cursing. Dalton adjusts his tie, smiles delightedly, then resumes his work with a satisfied air. Enter the two deputies, dragging in Vonda. Vonda is a good-looking woman, heavily made-up, in a short skirt, flashy colors—in short, a typical hooker.)

Vonda

Pigs, brutes, bastards! Haven't you any shame? To treat a woman like this? Let me go! Sons of bitches!

Dalton

What is it, what is it? What? You again?

Dobbs

Yes, Sheriff, this woman again. Parading her ass right up and down in front of Police Headquarters.

Dalton

In front of Police Headquarters, why—

Vonda

It's not true! You're a bunch of savages.

Dalton

Shut up! What's got into you? At this time of night and in that skirt? This is about the twentieth time you've been brought in here, isn't it?

Dobbs (to Vonda)

You'd be wise to keep your mouth shut.

Dillon

More, Sheriff. The thirtieth, at least.

Vonda

That's true.

Dalton

So, this is the way you take advantage of my good nature, my weakness?

Vonda

Let me go—you're hurting me. At least you could give me a smoke.

Dobbs (a raucous laugh)

Ha, ha—the sweet little thing.

Dillon (leering)

Come on, honey pie, you and me will go play in the cell.

Vonda

You are both pigs. Pigs!

Dalton

Shut up! Don't complicate your case. It's serious enough as it is.

Vonda

But, Sheriff, it's not my fault. These are savages.

Dalton

Shut up! (to the deputies)

Leave me along with her.

Dillon

Ah, Sheriff, she's just a slut.

Dobbs

And she's a real hellion, too. Might be dangerous.

Dalton

I'm not afraid. (to Vonda) I am going to deal with you once and for all. In front of Police Headquarters. You think I'm going to let you get away with that?

Vonda

I was just notching up my stocking.

Dillon

Every couple of minutes.

(Dillon imitates Vonda pulling up her skirt and notching up her stocking.)

Vonda (hotly)

It kept falling down.

Dalton

Resisting arrest and indecent behavior and soliciting police officers.

Vonda

I was not soliciting these pigs.

Dalton (to deputies)

She won't talk sensibly while you're around. You'd better go. (to Vonda) No resisting—understand?

Vonda

But, Mr. Sheriff—

(The deputies reluctantly go out.)

Dalton

Enough. What's your name? What's your name? Answer!

(The voices of the departing deputies fade slowly away. Vonda and the Sheriff look at each other and then break out in guffaws of laughter. Vonda throws herself onto his lap. They kiss voraciously.)

Vonda

Ah, my sweetheart, my sweetheart, my darling.

Dalton

She's always funny. Always a great actress. A riot! Good evening, my happy hooker. (gives her his hat) Your hat.

Vonda (putting on his hat, then mimicking him)

Shut up! What's your name? (kissing him) You are terrifying, aren't you?

(Dalton gets down on his knees and rocks in front of her.)

Vonda

No, no, don't do that.

Dalton

Come to mommy, come to mommy.

Vonda

No, no. They shook me up enough already.

Dalton

Poor little thing.

Vonda

And now, you know, I'm sure I've got black and blue marks all over my body.

Dalton (lewdly)

We'll see about that. (trying to undress her, but she evades him) Well, what's the matter?

Vonda

No, no. I've been manhandled enough, thank you. (she straightens herself up, rubs her arms and legs) Your deputies really worked me over, those brutes! They'd like to rape me. You'll see someday, they'll break something. And you call this love, do you?

Dalton

Love? Why, yes, ducky romantic love—love for our time. It brings to mind balconies and rope ladders, pimps and Ruffians—all in the moonlight. In this century, where we have no adventures, where life is so tepid, so flat. I find this delightful, unexpected—Shakespearean.

Vonda

What do you call it?

Dalton

I say it's Shakespearean.

Vonda

Police terminology. Really—

(Vonda becomes thoughtful, then sad.)

Dalton

Ravishing, ingenious little Vonda. What's the matter, baby?

Vonda

Nothing's wrong.

Dalton

Something ain't right. Come on.

Vonda

I—this isn't my idea of love.

Dalton

What's wrong with it?

Vonda

To dress up and act like a hooker, to get pushed around by those animals you call deputies. They make my flesh crawl.

Dalton

But, it's exciting, isn't it?

Vonda

Yes, it's exciting. I was amused at first. Now, well now, yes, it degrades me. (grimacing) It humiliates me. Pretty soon I'll have to spend a night in the slammer with some real hookers. So as to make it more romantic.

Dalton

It's a thought.

Vonda

Then, it will be with your deputies taking turns screwing me. Right? That would be Shakespearean. A gang-bang.

Dalton (liking the idea)

You exaggerate.

Vonda

So, that's it. I've had enough.

Dalton

You don't have any imagination, baby, that's why—no poetry. No love of the unusual. You're just not passionate.

Vonda

Me, not passionate? (outraged and hurt) Ah, honey, you remember.

Dalton

Yes, yes. I remember very well, sweetie. What I mean is, you lack cerebral passion. You've got it together physically, God knows, a little firepot. But you want regular love, clockwork romance. My God! Me, I want something unusual, the French Foreign Legion, struggle, danger, Romeo, Bogart—

Vonda (laughing)

Oh, you—

Dalton

Now, show me how you notched up your stocking.

Vonda (coyly)

Why, like this, honey. (she demonstrates in slow motion)

Dalton

I love it, I love it. I'll bet Dobbs wet his pants.

Vonda

They both looked like they were going to jump out of their skin. They kinda scare me, honey.

Dalton

Did they really hurt you?

Vonda

Did they ever.

Dalton (wildly)

And did you fight back?

Vonda

I kicked one of 'em in the balls, and scratched the other one.

Dalton (passionately excited)

Come on, come here, come here. (pulling her to the couch) Daddy's best girl. Are you wearing any panties tonight? I go crazy when you don't wear any panties.

Vonda

Find out for yourself. (after a weak resistance, allowing herself to be pulled down on the couch) Ok, ok. But listen, sweetheart, we've got to find a better way to see each other. You ought to have a better, a safer way. You, the Sheriff.

Dalton

There isn't any better way. This is the only way which satisfies my taste for adventure and at the same time affords me maximum security. I need security, you know. Not for me, but for my function. The Sheriff must be respected. I've got to set an example to the community. What do you expect? Besides, my wife is getting more and more jealous. She's watching me, spying on me, following me—all the time. I saw her face in a cab the other night when I was at the scene of a crime. Terrible. This is the only place I'm safe. In my office. She's capable of anything, anything, my wife.

Vonda

Your wife! Your wife! (looking at him closely) Wait a minute. Where've you been so late?

Dalton

The theatre.

Vonda

The theatre? Your wife? (crying) You don't love me.

Dalton (puzzled)

Why? Why don't I love you?

Vonda

No, you don't.

Dalton

But I adore you. Give me your lips.

Vonda

Oh, sure! You always want that! (turning her back on him)

Dalton (rapturously)

Your lips, your lips. I don't love you? But, if I didn't luv yuh, honey, why would I make you dress up like a hooker and expose you to the insults of my deputies, to worse, perhaps. Think a bit, unemotionally, coolly. These sacrifices ennoble the soul, purify the soul, they're sublime tests of love. A man doesn't impose tests like that on a woman he doesn't love passionately.

Vonda (impressed, but not really following his thinking)

You say so!

Dalton

Yes, I say so! Me, Jack Dalton, the Sheriff of this little one-horse town known as Atkinsville. Have you read de Sade? Have you read Genet? I say so because it is true. Drunkenness in humiliation. Pleasure in suffering. Suffering in pleasure.

Vonda

Lies!

Dalton

Whaddaya mean, lies? Psychological truth. Psychological and Christian, honey. What bothers me, what bothers me about you, honey, is that I have to explain all this to you. Other women, women who have read de Sade, they know this, they understand right away.

Vonda

Other women! (menacingly) What other women?

Dalton

I thought that would wake you up. Just getting a rise out of you, baby. Don't worry, I love you.

Vonda

You love me, perhaps, but you don't respect me. (Dalton makes protesting signs) No, you don't respect me. You want me to be a hooker. You don't respect me enough.

Dalton

Really, that's a little too much. You're crazy. See how unfeeling and unjust women are.

Vonda

No, no. (Dalton tries to kiss her) No, I came here to see my lover—like I was a criminal being dragged off to jail.

Dalton

Right. That's what's so exciting.

Vonda

Oh, for sure.

Dalton

Exciting, Shakespearean! I've passed you off before my deputies for a streetwalker, you, my adorable mistress.

And, I don't respect you? Talk sense.

Vonda

Jack!

Dalton

No, you see, it's discouraging and it's unworthy. But, my God! And who has ever shown you more respect than me? Me, with my elegant manners! Have I ever offered to pay you for your love?

Vonda

Of course not.

Dalton

Have I ever given you a penny—a single penny?

Vonda

That's true, but—

Dalton

Well, have I? There—(triumphantly) You see!

Vonda

Yes, but that's not the question.

Dalton

What, whaddaya mean, that's not the question? Of course, that's precisely the question.

Vonda

Say what you want. As for me, it infuriates me to be treated like this. I have some modesty. I assure you it takes away my pleasure. Why can't you come to me at my place?

Dalton

Impossible.

Vonda (coaxingly)

It's real nice at my place. I keep it real clean. And it doesn't smell like tobacco like this place, and I don't know what! Everything's under control. I'm a good housekeeper. Won't you—just once?

Dalton

Impossible.

Vonda

My mom will make us a nice dinner.

Dalton

No, no.

Vonda

Really. There's nothing to eat here. Come home with me—say you will.

Dalton

And my wife? Have you thought of that? If my wife found us together! Consider my wife's position. It would be a gross breach of trust in my marriage, and in my public life. What a situation.

Vonda (caressingly)

What? It would be funny, exciting—then, you could love me with a sense of real danger. It would be Shak—Shake—how do you say it?

Dalton

No, no—no more of this nonsense. This is madness. We're safer here. (grabbing her) Here, everything is under control, ha, ha.

Vonda

Let me go, leave me alone, you don't deserve any—

Dalton

What, me—me, with my cerebral passions—passionate, perverted? All right, perverted, I admit it. When you arrive with your clothes pulled loose, ruffled, torn, violated, struggling like a little bird in the big paws of my brave deputies—what do you want? It puts me in a rare mood. It makes my blood pound. (embracing her again)

Vonda

You disgust me. You're an egoist, a dirty old man. And don't give me any more shit. And, as for your wife—I don't give a damn about your wife! Are you really married? How am I to believe you?

Dalton (coaxingly)

Vonda!

Vonda

If you're married, where's her picture? All married men have their wife's pictures in their office.

Dalton

My wife doesn't like the way she photographs, that's all.

Vonda

And your theatre? The Sheriff's always at the theatre. I'll bet. As if it were natural.

Dalton

My duty requires me to be there to make sure there's nothing unsuitable being performed.

Vonda

Ah, your duty. It's really nice, your duty. You probably screw all the whores in town—right on this couch!

Dalton (injured innocence)

Vonda! You should know by now I would never touch a real whore.

Vonda

Let me be.

Dalton

Listen to me.

Vonda

I've had enough. Finished. You make me sick.

Dalton (drily)

You know me, my little Vonda, I don't like scenes. I have a horror of scenes. If I liked scenes, I'd stay home. I'd stay with my wife, who furnishes me with more scenes than I can count.

Vonda

Stay there then.

Dalton

Vonda.

Vonda

Shut up!

Dalton

Come on.

Vonda

I can't be bothered.

Dalton

You're wrong. I swear to you, you're wrong.

Vonda

Shit! Shit!

Dalton

I don't know to what excess anger can lead a Sheriff. (laughing nervously) Oh, ha, ha, ha—

(There is a noise of scuffling outside. They stop and listen.)

Dalton

Hmm, what can that be?

Vonda

Perhaps they're bringing you another one of your girlfriends.

Dalton

Shut up! (sitting at his desk) Go sit over there, adjust your skirt—and protest, rebel. Quickly, quickly. Don't be afraid to rebel. Call me names. I love names. Hurl 'em at me. Be nasty, abuse me. Hurry up—look sharp.

Vonda

You really want me to?

Dalton

Hell yes! Come on.

(The door opens and the deputies enter, pulling in Mitch Powell.)

Dalton (to Vonda)

Shut up, shut up. You are insolent. Will you kindly be quiet!

Vonda

It's not true! They lied. They are animals, savages, murderers. And you are, too. You're a brute, a dirty old man. Pig! Pig! Pig!

Dalton

Good! Fine. Shut up. When will you tell me your name? I forbid you to speak to me like that.

Vonda

Skunk.

(The deputies release their prisoner and are ready to hurl themselves on Vonda. She defies them with clenched fists.)

Dobbs

Put her in a cell!

Dillon

Let me work her over with my belt, chief. I'll teach her some respect.

Dobbs

A dildo's what she needs.

Vonda

You need one, too.

Dalton

Leave this woman. I am not finished with her. She's got the devil in her.—Now, what's this? What's he done? What's he in for? Nasty-looking brute. (to Mitch Powell) What makes you prowl the streets at this time of night?

Mitch

It's not that late for a poor man.

Sheriff

Not late, not late? What are you talking about? Shut up, and don't joke with me. Why didn't you book him?

Dobbs

This man is perfectly free.

Dalton

Just because he came in freely, doesn't mean he can leave freely.

Dobbs

He asked to see you on a matter of urgency.

Dalton

On a matter of urgency? Really! And if all the criminals in town asked to see me urgently at two in the morning, while I'm engaged in important business, I suppose you'd bring them here to my office?

Dobbs

But chief—(to Mitch after some nodding) Leave me alone, you. Settle down. (pushing Mitch)

Dalton

Come on, talk. What do you want here? Make it quick.

Mitch

Pardon me, excuse me, Sheriff. I only wanted to tell you—

Dalton

You want to tell me. You want to tell me. What do you want to tell me?

Mitch

Sir, I have something. I brought you something. I found it…very unusual. I found it not ten minutes ago, right in front of Police Headquarters.

(Mitch looks at Vonda and smiles.)

Dalton

In front of Police Headquarters? It's frightening, the things they find in the street in front of Police Headquarters.

Vonda

Talk all you like—skunk.

Dobbs

That woman is going to get some old-fashioned police brutality.

Dalton

Let her alone, let her alone. I am taking notes. Now, what did you find (scornfully) on the street?

Mitch (pulling out a wallet)

Here, sir.

Dalton

Just a wallet. I thought it must be something special, like a diamond ring or something.

Mitch

A wallet, Mr. Sheriff, a red leather wallet with money in it.

Dalton (smirking)

But, only a few dollars, of course.

(The Sheriff and the deputies laugh.)

Mitch

See for yourself. I haven't touched a penny.

Dalton

You bother me at two in the morning over a billfold! (opening it) If there's nothing here—watch out! Let's see, let's see. This is crazy, this is impossible. (Mitch gives a series of approving nods and smiles to the deputies, who return them with furious looks and gestures) Wow! This is a fairy tale. Ten thousand dollars. (recounting) Word of honor—ten thousand dollars.

Mitch

Ten thousand dollars. It's all there, yes indeed, yes indeed.

Dalton

Good Lord, it's an enormous sum, enormous—a fortune. Holy-moly!

Mitch

When I think there are actually people who go strolling around with that much money, while the rest of us—

Dalton

And you actually found this?

Mitch

Indeed I did, sir.

Dalton

That's really astounding. I didn't think there was anybody in Atkinsville that had that much money.

Vonda

It's Shake, Shake—

Dillon

You shut up.

Dobbs

This doesn't concern hookers.

Dalton (to deputies)

Never mind, never mind. (to Mitch) Please tell us how you found it.

Mitch

It was easy, sir. Here's what happened. I was near the theatre—

Dalton

Oh, you're a first-nighter like me, eh?

Mitch

I only wish. I just happened to be in the neighborhood. But there were so many people, and I was tired. My hernia was acting up. I've got a hernia that causes me a lot of trouble, Sheriff, and I'm not very agile. From military service. So, anyway, I saw this well-dressed dude who was a bit drunk—four sheets to the wind, actually. That man wouldn't give a poor beggar like me the time of day. A man without pity. A millionaire, I guess.

Dalton

Unfortunate, no doubt. But, what can the rich do for the poor anyway? Don't slander millionaires, my dear sir. Millionaires are indispensable to society.

Vonda

There aren't nearly enough of them to go around, in my opinion.

Dobbs

Shut up!

Dalton

She's absolutely right. The government should concentrate its efforts at social reform on the object of producing more millionaires instead of giving money to the poor. If it weren't for millionaires, you wouldn't be finding any wallets like this one. So—go on.

Mitch

Well, I wished him to hell, I assure you. Actually, I suppose it's all the fault of Osama bin Laden—

Dalton

Bin Laden, everything's the fault of Osama bin Laden.

Mitch

May God get him for all the trouble he's causing.

Dalton

Right, right. But let's get down to business.

Mitch

I'm getting to it, Sheriff.

Dalton

Hurry up, finish, come on.

Mitch

Well, I wanted to get a cup of coffee. I was more or less behind this rich dude, but limping along a ways back because of my hernia.

Dalton

Kindly get to the point.

Mitch

Well, he's a little bit ahead of me—and he hails a cab. As he's getting in, I notice he drops something. I give a shout, but the cab pulls out. By the time I limp up, all I see is this billfold. Naturally, I had a look at it. And I saw what you see. And the street's empty. Absolutely empty. And there I am with ten thousand dollars in my hand. Never before in all my life did I realize what it is to be poor. And yet I've always been poor. And nothing else in the billfold. No identification, nothing. Not even a picture. So you see, I was scrounging for money for a cup of coffee and I fell over ten thousand dollars—little good it does me. I walked on over here—it was on my way.

Vonda

How interesting! What a fathead!

(Dobbs shakes his fist at Vonda.)

Mitch

And now, Mr. Sheriff, it's late and I'd like to be on my way. I have an engagement.

Dalton

Just a minute. You can't go like that. Nosiree, not like that. That's an amazing story you've told me. A fairy tale. It's Shakespearean! But, my God, if all this is true—

Mitch

Every word is true, sir.

Dalton

I believe you, I believe you. It has to be true. No one would make something like this up. But holy cow—you're an honest man. A hero. There's no getting out of it, you're a hero of our times.

Mitch

I'm no hero.

Dalton

No mistake. Don't argue with me. I'm convinced of it. I'll tell everybody. This man is a hero.

Mitch

But sir, suppose a policemen found the wallet?

Dobbs

Hmm—wow!

Dillon

Would I like that.

Mitch

Or even this pretty lady?

Vonda

Hey, you're a nice gentleman, more than I can say for some people.

Mitch

Or even you, Sheriff?

Dalton

Me! The hell! Well, then I'd be a hero, too. A hero, like you, understand? Even it if was my duty. I don't take back a word. Ten grand! My Lord. And the street was deserted—you could have easily—

Mitch

But my leg isn't too good, you know.

Dalton

Don't say that. Don't slander yourself. This is a fine thing, splendid, heroic. I can't find the right word for it. You should get the medal of honor or something, really, or maybe a Nobel Prize. This is the biggest thing that's ever happened in Atkinsville, in as long as I can remember. What's your name?

Mitch

Mitch Powell.

Dalton

Mitch Powell. Mitch Powell. Marvelous, Mitch Powell. This belongs in a book. What do you do for a living? Mitch?

Mitch

Huh?

Dalton

What do you do? What kind of work? Your profession?

Mitch

Well—

Dalton

Finding wallets is not your regular job.

Mitch

I'm afraid it's the only one I have.

Dalton (astonished)

What—you don't work?

Mitch

It's obvious to look at me, isn't it? I used to be a waiter, but I can't do that any more cause I can't move fast enough on account of my hernia.

Dalton

You get a disability pension?

Mitch

They say I'm not sufficiently disabled. But nobody will hire me. I get public assistance.

Dalton (icily)

You mean welfare?

Mitch

I guess that's what you call it.

Dalton

You mean you're one of them welfare cheats? (disappointed) And I thought so highly of you.

Mitch

I ain't happy about it. I'd be happy to work if someone would hire me.

Dalton

Sure, sure. They all say that. Where do you live?

Mitch

Good Hope Park.

Dalton (surprised)

Oh, that's a nice neighborhood. You live with relatives, I suppose. What number?

Mitch

No number. At least I never saw one on the grate.

Dalton

You're kidding.

Mitch

Unfortunately, no. A grate is the last word in modern living conveniences, Sheriff.

Dalton

Then, you have no place to live?

Mitch

Homeless!

Dalton

That's terrible! Really terrible! But you have to have a place to live.

Mitch

I've been saying that myself.

Dalton

Don't try to be funny. You're no comedian. Do you know what it is to be homeless?

Mitch

I'm perfectly well acquainted with it—with every aspect of it. It's a misfortune.

Dalton

It's not a misfortune, it's a crime. It is not allowed in this town. We don't permit homeless persons in our fair city.

Dalton

Well, I'm perfectly willing to change my present situation for a better one.

Dalton

Homelessness—homeless people in a town. It's like a social cancer. You're a dangerous man, Mitch Powell.

Mitch

Me, dangerous? I'm an old man with a hernia that I can't afford to get fixed.

Dalton

A hernia. A hernia is nothing to do with it. Who cares whether you've got a hernia or not. You haven't got a home. People without homes are vagabonds. You are guilty of being a tramp. This is very annoying and complicated. There's no law in favor of heroes—but the City Council has an ordinance against vagabonds. A whole heap of laws against vagabonds.

Mitch

I believe it. There's always something.

Dalton

You didn't think of that when you found the billfold, did you? You were only thinking of being a hero, of glory—

Mitch

Really, sir—

Dalton

Shut up! What a naïve idea!

Mitch

If I'd known the law, I'd have let someone else do it.

Dalton

That would have been the best thing to do, by far. The rich take their wealth where they find it—why did you have to be different?

Mitch

I'm a poor man.

Dalton

Right. Your reasoning is sound. But, what a misfortune.

Mitch

I thought maybe honesty would be important.

Dalton

It's not a question of being honest. No one asks you to be honest, Mitch. The only thing the law says is don't break the law. You can be as dishonest as you like, provided you don't break the law—

Vonda

Or get caught!

Dalton

It's solely a question of respecting the law or getting around it, which is the same thing.

Mitch

Right, right. But you have to have money to do that.

Dalton

What do you want? Look at it this way. Here's this billfold. In your place, in your situation—it was a fine thing to return it, I agree. I don't mean to say you were an imbecile to do it. No, on the contrary, morally speaking, your action is quite meritorious—awe-inspiring—and even worthy of a reward. A hundred dollars at least. If the owner is ever found, I am sure he would agree. Yes, but legally, legally, you are in a very bad fix.

Mitch

I understand, I understand.

Dalton

There simply isn't any law obliging you to go around finding billfolds. See—here's the City Code. Look at it, if you like.

Mitch

I believe you.

Dalton

However, there are numerous and explicit provisions—penalties—for being a vagabond. You would have been much better off to find a home than this wallet.

Mitch

I couldn't agree more.

Dalton

I am going to find you a home.

Mitch (surprised)

Really?

Dalton

Word of honor.

Mitch

It's really kind of you—

Dalton

Right here—

Mitch

In your house?

Dalton

You'll be my guest for the night.

Mitch

Thank you, Sheriff.

Dalton

And tomorrow morning, I'm going to put you on the first train.

Mitch

The first train?

Dalton

Right.

Vonda

Hey, you can't do that—nobody does that anymore, it's illegal.

Mitch

My God!

Dalton

Arrest this man. But go easy with him. He's a hero.

Vonda

It's unconstitutional—

Dobbs and Dillon (brutally)

Come on. We've got a nice little cell for you. (dragging him off) Out you go!

Mitch

But, you can't do this. The lady is right, the Supreme Court has said—

Dalton

Are you some kind of liberal or commie? Don't mention that un-American institution to me.

Dillon

Out you go, bum. You can talk later.

Dobbs

Some kind of hero.

Mitch

Please—

(Dobbs and Dillon drag Mitch out.)

Vonda

It's despicable. Is that your idea of a joke?

Dalton

What? Not in the least.

Vonda

You're not going to run him out of town?

Dalton

I sure am.

Vonda

How can you?

Dalton

Got to. We can't have homeless people in this town. Give the place a bad name.

Vonda

Oh, no! You are DETESTABLE! DETESTABLE!

Dalton

No need to talk like that, now. Nobody's around, baby.

Vonda

This time it's for your benefit. And I mean it. I don't want you anymore. I am ashamed of you. God, you're ugly.

Dalton

You know, you're getting on my nerves.

Vonda

Oh, am I? Well, I've just begun.

Dalton

Have you? Do me a favor, and get out of here.

Vonda

No, I'm not going. I'm going to give you a piece of my mind.

Dalton

You don't want to leave?

Vonda

No, no!

Dalton

As you please.

(Dalton pushes a button.)

Vonda

What are you doing?

Dalton

You'll see.

(Dobbs and Dillon come in.)

Dalton

Lay hands on this woman.

Vonda (spluttering in rage)

You, you—you—

Dalton (calmly)

And put her in a cell.

Vonda

What—?

Dalton

With the other hookers. I'll see about her in the morning.

Dillon

That's not bad.

Dobbs

It's a nice cell.

(Dobbs and Dillon pin Vonda's arms.)

Vonda

No, no. I don't want it.

Dobbs

Maybe I'll come see you there, honey.

Dillon

Don't want you to be lonely.

Dobbs

We're very hospitable around here.

Vonda

Let me go. I don't want it. I don't want it.

Dillon

You're going to get it, honey. Tonight.

Vonda

Brutes, animals, no, no!

Dobbs

Shut up, you little bitch. You've got a lesson to learn.

Dalton

Be easy on her, boys. She's a woman after all.

Dobbs

There won't be any bruises.

Vonda

I'll expose you. I'll tell everybody about you. I'll tell your wife.

(Dobbs and Dillon pull Vonda off, screaming.)

Dalton (alone)

My wife's been dead for years. (walks up and down, takes the billfold, looks at it, then locks it in a safe) Imbecile!

(lighting a cigarette) These crazy women. You can't have eight days peace in a row with them—no, not ever. Why should she care what happens to this vagabond? What a disgusting way to spend the evening. Well, it was time to get rid of her. Still, maybe I should stop Dobbs. He's a real sadist, and might—

(Enter Sergeant Chambers.)

Chambers

Excuse me, Sheriff, but—

Dalton

You—but what—what are you doing here?

Chambers (bewildered, hearing Vonda screaming off stage)

Sir—

Dalton

Are you going to get out of here?

Chambers

But Sheriff Dalton, I forgot—it was stupid of me, but I forgot my house keys and—

Dalton

Get out and leave me in peace, or I am going to put you in a cell, too.

(Dobbs and Dillon return, grinning.)

Dalton

And you get out, too.

(The Sheriff beats them all as the curtain falls.)

CURTAIN

LADY LIBERTY
A PLAY IN ONE ACT, ADAPTED FROM A PLAY BY HENRI DUVERNOIS

CAST OF CHARACTERS:

Bernard, an artist

Marsha, his wife

Henry the VIII

Dr. Watson

Lattimore

THE PLAY

The action takes place in Dr. Watson's Sanatorium sometime in the twentieth century.

A comfortable room in Dr. Watson's sanatorium; there are chairs and a small bed. Bernard is at an easel, painting. Bernard is singing lustily. A knock.

Bernard (easily)

C'mon in. (greeting Henry the VIII with a friendly gesture; Bernard is used to Henry and relishes his company) Ah, will Milord be good enough to enter?

Henry

Good morrow, my dear Duke.

Bernard (cheerfully)

Good morrow, your Highness.

Henry (regally gracious)

Don't put yourself out! Carry on. You sing while you paint.

Bernard

Yes, Milord. Like a Volga boatman.

Henry

Proof of a pure heart.

(Henry inspects the work on the easel. The picture is all lines and blots.)

Henry

Landscape?

Bernard

Landscape.

Henry

Charming.

Bernard (bowing)

Your patronage, Milord, flatters and honors me.

Henry

Charming. We have always taken care to make England first in art—it shall always be our royal care to reward artists. That is why I made you a Duke.

Bernard

The world needs more monarchs like you, Your Majesty.

Henry

Is it finished?

Bernard

Does Your Majesty like it this way?

Henry

Quite.

Bernard

Then, if you approve, I have nothing more to do than sign it. (signing it)

Henry

Now, the delicate question: how much?

Bernard

Four hundred pounds—for you, Your Majesty.

Henry

Say five hundred in round figures. I will buy it for Anne Boleyn. Is it dry?

Bernard

Not for a day or so.

Henry

That's too bad! I want to go this evening.

Bernard

Your Majesty has decided to leave us?

Henry

My duty calls. Cardinal Wolsey has written me in cipher. My bags are packed. Let the coach be brought.

Bernard

What a shame! You'll miss the festivities. There's going to be an artists' ball—

Henry (pompously)

My Lord Duke, those who are called to grand affairs because of the misfortune of their birth must leave little joys for great cares. You have the best of it. Artists live in an Eden that even Kings cannot enter. Bah, I must look at budgets and state papers. There are times when I envy men such as you (but probably not often).

Bernard (touched)

Oh, Milord—

Henry

Yes, yes, I swear to you—uneasy lies the head that wears the crown—uneasy and bored.

(Enter Dr. Watson. White coat, businesslike, short beard like Dr. Freud, whom he fancies he resembles and tries to resemble whether he does or not.)

Bernard

Ah, Dr. Watson.

Watson

I believe Your Majesty is wanted—

Henry

We leave for Portsmouth tonight. But that's a state secret, mind.

Watson (absently, not much interested in Henry)

Yes.

Henry

I have no time. Fare thee well, Duke Bernard.

Bernard (bowing)

My humble duty, Your Highness.

Henry (something has clicked off or on in Henry's mind)

I have an excellent souvenir of you. At first I had a prejudice against you. Then I saw you had the most beautiful bird's nest in your beard.

Bernard (dumbfounded)

Huh?

Henry

One would think you were speaking. Not so! It's the bird singing—tweet, tweet, tweet-tweet. To reward you, noble Bernard, I name you Captain General of the Order of the Knights of Malta.

Bernard

A thousand thanks.

Henry

Think nothing of it. It's a little red cross with a green ribbon.

Bernard

Delighted.

Henry

Kneel and kiss my ring.

Watson

Come on, that's enough.

Henry

Kiss my ring, wretch!

Watson

Go back to your room immediately, Mr. Simpson.

Henry

I will deprive you of all your titles, Cardinal Wolsey.

Watson

That's understood. Now be off.

Henry

I'll have your head off. You don't respect the Pope. You infidel. I'll burn you at the stake.

Watson

You cannot be both Henry the Eighth and also be the Pope. Now, make up your mind who you are, Mr. Simpson.

Henry

Why can't I?

Watson

Why can't you what?

Henry

Why can't I be Pope, too?

Watson

We simply don't permit multiple delusions in this institution, Mr. Simpson. It's hard enough to handle one.

Henry

What's the use of being crazy if one can't do what one likes? (stamping his foot) I demand my right to be whoever I please, whenever I please.

Watson (icily)

If you insist on being difficult, Mr. Simpson, I will arrange to send you to a state institution where they permit all sorts of behavior, and you may have as many delusions as you like. (a terrible silence) Now, go find Anne Boleyn!

Henry (exits, cringing, but after he leaves his courage comes back somewhat)

To hell with those who do not comprehend me. A WHORE! A WHORE! MY KINGDOM FOR A WHORE!

Bernard

Poor fellow. Each morning he says he's leaving in the evening, but he never does. Still, he always buys my pictures.

Watson

He's a very difficult case. Now Dr. Freud says about this kind of delusion that—

Bernard

Excuse me, Dr. Watson—but why can't he?

Watson (puzzled)

Why can't he what?

Bernard

Why can't he have more than one delusion?

Watson

You've got to draw the line somewhere, you know. It's the first step to a cure—

Bernard (comprehending)

Ah—

Watson

And Dr. Freud says—

Bernard

You know, Dr. Watson, you resemble him.

Watson

I resemble—?

Bernard

Dr. Freud.

Watson (delighted)

Do you think so?

Bernard

Absolutely.

Watson (even more delighted)

You're just saying that.

Bernard

Not at all.

Watson

I admire him so much. I like to think I follow in the master's footsteps. That's what accounts for it.

Bernard

The resemblance is extraordinary.

Watson

You're just trying to get around me. I can't let you do that. How are you coming along today?

Bernard

Me? Very good. (sighing) Except that I'm a bell, Dr. Watson.

Watson

Oh? I don't think Dr. Freud ever had a patient who thought he was a bell. A wolf—he had a patient who thought he was a wolf.

Bernard

I'm not a wolf.

Watson

That complicates matters.

Bernard

Although my wife said I was.

Watson

Perhaps you dreamed about being a wolf.

Bernard

Never. I never was a wolf and I never dreamed about being one.

Watson

You're not being very helpful.

Bernard

On even days, I'm a bell.

Watson (disgusted)

A bell still.

Bernard (indignantly)

Not just any bell.

Watson

You're a special bell?

Bernard

The Liberty Bell.

Watson (hopefully)

And on odd days?

Bernard

On odd days, I'm parchment.

Watson (unable to restrain his disappointment)

Shit!

Bernard

No, not toilet paper: parchment.

Watson (furious, with great contempt)

The Declaration of Independence, perhaps?

Bernard (pleasantly)

Not at all. The Magna Carta.

Watson

It's unusual. Most of my patients think they're someone else.

Bernard

Like Simpson, who thinks he's Henry the Eighth?

Watson

Exactly.

Bernard

But I know exactly who I am. I am Bernard Peterson and I live at 1182 Nicholson Lane. I'm a painter by profession. I am married and thirty-eight-years old. My wife is a journalist. You see, I know who I am.

Watson

Yes.

Bernard

It's just that sometimes I'm a bell and sometimes I'm parchment.

Watson

Yes. Instead of thinking you're someone else, you think you're something else.

Bernard

You've got it.

Watson

And you're not just one thing.

Bernard

Precisely.

Watson

Instead of a split personality, you have a split substance, as it were, a dual substantiality, as a philosopher might say.

Bernard

It's very disconcerting.

Watson

Is it?

Bernard

Well, of course. To know who you are, but not what you are.

Watson

Have you ever dreamed that—?

Bernard

I never remember my dreams, Dr. Freud. (Watson smiles) I mean, Dr. Watson—please forgive—

Watson (beaming)

Think nothing of it. A natural mistake. (looking at the painting) Perhaps we can get at your inner thoughts through your art. (Watson is speaking more and more with a Viennese accent) You're not a modern eccentric, I can see that. Now tell me what you think this represents, ach?

Bernard

A pure tone! Like a bell. It's meant to describe resonance. Resonance abounding.

Watson

Ach, ach—So, now we are getting somewhere. And this reminds you of making love to your mother, nein?

Bernard

Nein. It reminds me of innocence.

Watson

Hmmm! You're a tough one, a very tough one. By the way, one of your colleagues is here to see you. That's what I came to tell you, but I forgot.

Bernard (cagily)

He can come in. But tell him to speak softly.

Watson

Why? So as not to disturb your dreams about your mother?

Bernard

No, no. A bell is a very sensitive instrument. I don't want to acquire any more cracks, you know.

Watson

Ach—

Bernard

I might break.

Watson

You know, you're never going to get better so long as you keep denying your relationship to your mother. Why not confess to me—

Bernard

Who is it?

Watson (slowly)

Lattimore. (watching him closely) A friend of yours. (triumphantly) And of your mother's!

Bernard

How could I forget old Lattimore! Poor fellow's a miserable married man.

Watson

No reason to abuse him. You're jealous, of course.

(Bernard stares at Watson.)

Watson

Because of his relationship to your mother.

Bernard

Nonsense. It's the simple truth.

Watson

Why speak the simple truth about someone for no reason? Nobody does that. You must have a reason. You hate him because your mother liked him—

Bernard

My mother did not especially like him.

Watson

The first phase is always denial. (looking at his watch) Your fifty minutes is up for today. I will send your friend to you. Best not to go into this business about being a bell or a parchment. He's a bit impressionable, and rather uneasy about being in a place like this. Very nervous. Can I count on your discretion?

Bernard

Of course.

Watson (going out)

Come in, Mr. Lattimore.

Lattimore (enters warily, looks around, checking for a way to escape)

It's me, Bernie.

Watson

I'll leave you.

Lattimore (uneasy)

You're not going to leave us, are you, Doctor?

Watson

You must have many things to discuss.

Lattimore (nervously)

Not really.

Bernard

Really.

Lattimore

Err—hello, Bernie.

Bernard

I'm a bell, a sonorous bell.

Lattimore (stepping behind the doctor)

Hello, Bell. Really, you won't leave us, Doctor? I can only stay a minute—and—and—I might upset the pa—I mean I might lose my way and not be able to find my way out.

Watson (disengaging himself)

Just ring. An orderly will come and let you out. Tomorrow, Bernard—Mr. Lattimore. (escaping from Lattimore)

Lattimore (in a weak voice)

Really, Doc—you ought to stay. (desperately) Doc!

(Exit Watson.)

Bernard

Good to see you, Vic.

Lattimore (with patently false bonhomie)

Ah, you recognize me. You look fine, old boy. Fine. I brought you some popcorn—would you like some?

Bernard

I hate popcorn.

Lattimore (confused)

But Marsha always said you loved popcorn.

Bernard

Marsha loved popcorn. She was always stuffing me with it.

Lattimore (edging towards the door)

Oh.

Bernard

She bought it for herself. But, thanks all the same. I never expected to see you. Splendid of you.

Lattimore (sounding unnatural)

We're old friends, aren't we? It's natural.

Bernard

And daring!

Lattimore

Daring?

Bernard

For you.

Lattimore

Look, there's no reason to be like that just because you don't like the popcorn. Next time I'll bring—ah—ah, M&M's.

Bernard

Don't be so frightened, you idiot.

Lattimore

Me, frightened? Why should I be frightened? Ridiculous, me frightened.

Bernard (looking around craftily)

Shh! Wait. (peeking behind the door) Nobody's listening.

Lattimore (to himself, terrified)

Crazy as a coot.

(Bernard places his hand on Lattimore's shoulder. Lattimore cringes.)

Bernard

Look, Vic, I'm sorry for you. I told you not to be afraid.

Lattimore (wildly)

I'm not afraid, I'm not afraid.

Bernard (secretively)

I'm not crazy. Shh!

Lattimore (jelly-like)

Of course not.

Bernard

Vic, I swear to you that I am not crazy.

Lattimore

You're a little eccentric—like most artists—that's all. A little rest—a little electric shock.

Bernard

Let me prove it to you.

Lattimore

Oh, don't bother.

Bernard

Vic, I know I'm not a bell. I'm like you and everybody else. Flesh and blood. Fully conscious. I'm giving Dr. Watson, who really thinks he's Dr. Freud, a crock of shit. Don't you believe me?

Lattimore

I believe you! I believe you.

Bernard

Bah! You're humoring me.

Lattimore

Don't be unfair, Bernie. I came here to find out how you are. You had a (searching for an appropriate euphemism) crisis—not really a breakdown. It's over. Very soon, I'll come back and take you home.

Bernard

No way!

Lattimore

No way? You know where you are?

Bernard

In Dr. Watson's Sanatorium.

Lattimore

Well then?

Bernard

Have a cigarette. I'm going to light up and enlighten you, but only if you promise to keep my secret. Word of honor.

Lattimore

Scout's oath.

Bernard

What do you think of the place?

Lattimore (appraisingly)

Nice—very nice—as such places go.

Bernard

Isn't it? It's quiet. Orderlies are o.k., if you tip them. It's like an artists' colony.

Lattimore

And the weirdoes?

Bernard

Bah! You always meet a few weirdoes in life. Most of them are outside, you know. And they're usually more dangerous. Here I've got relationships. There's an old guy who thinks he's Henry the Eighth. He just made me a Knight of Malta—Commander, I think—and he always buys my paintings. I never thought about being a Knight of Malta. Sounds good to me. Who wants to be like everybody else?

Lattimore

But this Henry the Eighth is a wacko.

Bernard

I don't deny that. But some of my best friends are wackos. (gesture from Lattimore) Wackos are just like everybody else—except they're not ashamed to pretend their dreams are real.

Lattimore

You don't mind being surrounded by nuts?

Bernard

Not at all. They're nice people, especially if you go along with their little games.

Lattimore

I don't see why you find life here so attractive that you don't want to leave.

Bernard

Because I'm perfectly free here. Nobody bothers me. Get that—nobody!

Lattimore

Bernie, listen, I'll admit I was afraid coming to see you at this funny farm. But you're just like you always were. You've been ill—a breakdown—a thing that's over and done with. I'll have you out of here by morning, I swear it.

Bernard

You always were dense, Vic. I have no intention of leaving.

Lattimore

No intention of leaving?

Bernard

None at all.

Lattimore

You want to stay here?

Bernard

That's what I'm telling you. That's what I've been telling you.

Lattimore

Why?

Bernard

Because otherwise I'd have to go home to Marsha.

Lattimore

Well, no wonder. Of course, it's Marsha. (as if he understands completely) I don't blame you a bit.

Bernard

Marsha. Brr! The very name gives me a chill. Look—understand. If I'm crazy, I can remain here at peace, and alone. If I'm cured, if I admit I'm not sick, then I have to go back to see her, to listen to her, to live with her. I haven't seen her in six months. And for six months I've been happy!

Lattimore

Happy?

Bernard

Do you know what happy means?

Lattimore

Well, I used to think I did, but I'm not so sure any more. What is happiness, Bernie?

Bernard

Happiness is a room—any room—without Marsha.

Lattimore

You mean that you're staying here of your own free will?

Bernard

Of my own glorious, free, unencumbered will! I can breathe. I've never been more free. You remember what Marsha was like?

Lattimore

Yes.

Bernard

How she cried.

Lattimore (considering)

She did cry a lot.

Bernard

How she liked to fight—over nothing.

Lattimore

She did fight a lot.

Bernard

How she got jealous.

Lattimore

She did get jealous.

Bernard

She gave me terrible headaches. I couldn't work.

Lattimore

Why didn't you get a divorce?

Bernard

How could I divorce her? After all, I was in love with her.

Lattimore

But, after what you just said—

Bernard

I didn't say I didn't love her. She drove me crazy, that's all.

Lattimore

I think I understand. She was loyal, charming, chaste—

Bernard

All the more admirable since no one suspected her of it.

Lattimore

Don't blaspheme.

Bernard

I can say what I want in this place. Anyway, one day I failed in a suicide attempt.

Lattimore

Are you putting me on?

Bernard

No. But I couldn't do it. I felt my life was useless. And useless for me to live with Marsha. And yet, I love life. I'm a creator, an artist, and life provides so many opportunities. I'm never bored. I even like silence. But ever since I've lived with Marsha, my ears have been tortured with her constant whinings and complainings. I was condemned to Marsha for life. Then I had an idea. I read about this place in the papers.

Lattimore

All the advantages of a prison with none of the inconveniences.

Bernard

And the fair prospect of finishing the rest of my life without disturbance from my wife. So, one morning, as Marsha was putting on her make-up—

Lattimore

You told her you were Napoleon Bonaparte.

Bernard

No, no. Marsha is Jewish. I told her I was Adolf Hitler. And bit by bit I added little embellishments.

Lattimore

And how did she react to that? It was a low blow.

Bernard

She said: "Stop kidding around."

Lattimore

It didn't work?

Bernard

It took time. I kept telling her that I was fantasizing about decapitating women—and that I wanted her to assist me.

Lattimore

What did she say to that?

Bernard

She said: "Get dressed or we're going to have trouble." It wasn't easy, but I kept it up for several days. I refused to put on my clothes. Finally, she was convinced I was having a breakdown. And so, here I am in paradise.

Lattimore

But what about Marsha?

Bernard

They let her come to see me twice a week now. For ten minutes. If she stays longer, I start acting funny and they make her go. In fact, she's going to be here soon. She brings me cigarettes and candy. While I rave she unburdens herself of her little domestic anecdotes. We don't listen to each other. We sort of make noises in each other's presence. That's the way it always was—only now it only lasts ten minutes twice a week. Then she packs up and I appreciate this place even more.

Lattimore

I wonder how I'd like it here? And you never intend to leave?

Bernard

What for?

Lattimore

What for? (thoughtfully) And your doctor?

Bernard

Dr. Watson comes to see me. I ask him about Sherlock Holmes. He laughs, starts talking about Dr. Freud. He asks me how I feel. I tell him just like a bell. Sound as a bell. I leave it at that. I don't improve. I don't get worse. And he's happy. If I got worse, he'd be upset. So I am always the same. Speaking of someone who is always the same, how's the missus?

Lattimore

She comes and goes—comes and goes—frequently. (musing) Is it expensive here?

Bernard

Not for me. My health insurance pays for most of it.

Lattimore

Interesting. Who's your carrier?

Bernard

Metropolitan.

Lattimore (plainly delighted)

By jingo! I'm covered by Metropolitan, too!

Bernard

I probably shouldn't have told you—

Lattimore

Why not, why not? I'm your best friend, right? Why should there be any secrets? Especially about a matter of such—err, vital concern—to one's mental health, peace of mind, and all that. The entrance exam doesn't seem to be difficult. (looking around) It really is nice here!

Bernard

There's an empty room across the hall. (knocking) Someone's coming— (furtively) Mum's the word.

Lattimore (grasping Bernard's hand conspiratorially)

Mum's the word, old buddy. I'm going.

Bernard

Dum de dum dum. (slyly) It's Marsha. COME IN!

(Enter Marsha, a woman a little younger than Bernard. Not bad-looking in a domestic sort of way, but a woman who does not care too much for her appearance.)

Marsha (not very friendly)

Well, I didn't expect to meet you today, Mr. Lattimore.

Lattimore (cordially)

Delighted. Hope you are in good health.

Bernard (sensing trouble)

A bell. Bong! Bong! BONG!

Marsha (suspicious, she suspects she's being kept in the dark)

Why did you come here?

Lattimore (innocently)

To see Bernie.

Marsha (with implied menace)

You shouldn't stay long. He needs rest.

Bernie (with a conspiratorial wink)

BONG!

Lattimore

I'm just going.

Bernie

Bong! BONG!

Marsha

Well, I hope to see you again (meaning, not for a good long while, Mr. Lattimore) But—things are so difficult when one is married. (bringing up a sore point) Does your wife still like to dance?

Lattimore (wincing)

Always!

Marsha (sweetly)

She's energetic.

Bernie

Silence everyone, I'm going to peal!

Lattimore

Bye, old buddy. See you soon.

Marsha

Soon? No.

Bernie

Please give my humble service to Her Majesty, the Queen of Poland—when next you see her.

Lattimore (with a wink to Marsha implying Bernie is crazy)

And (a covert conspiratorial wink to Bernie) I won't forget. Good evening, Marsha.

(Exit Lattimore.)

Marsha (not necessarily waiting to find out if Lattimore is out of earshot)

Good riddance! I can't stand that man. Do you want me to tell you why?

Bernie (with great detachment)

Not at all.

Marsha (paying not the slightest attention)

You see, I know about his wife.

Bernie (trying to disconcert her)

The Queen of Poland?

Marsha

A woman's sin is always the same as a man's. I can speak freely because I've never fooled around on you myself.

Bernie (gritting his teeth)

Careful!

Marsha

What?

Bernie

A false note and I might shatter.

Marsha

You irritate me.

Bernie

We'll see about that. B O N G!

Marsha (hastily)

Now, don't go off on me. Here, I brought you your candy and cigarettes.

Bernie

Thank you, O Beauteous Queen of Sheba.

Marsha (shrugging her shoulders)

The Queen of Sheba now.

Bernie (backing away)

Don't get too close.

Marsha

Are you a bell today?

Bernie

You might shatter me.

Marsha (angrily)

They've got to put your head back together again. Who put that crazy idea in your head that you're some kind of a bell?

Bernie

It's not crazy. Bong. Bong. Can't you see I'm a bell. Listen up, woman.

Marsha

And tomorrow you'll be some sort of parchment?

Bernie

Likely.

Marsha (annoyed)

But, you fool, if you were a bell or a parchment, you wouldn't be alive. You wouldn't be married to me.

Bernie

That's easy for you to say. (significantly) I know! I'm the only one who really knows what's going on. What do you suppose you really are?

Marsha (astounded)

Me? I'm me, of course.

Bernie

No, Marsha. You're lipstick.

Marsha

Lipstick. You're crazy. You never could carry on a conversation, but now you're totally impossible. You never ask me how things are going at home. (Bernie smiles knowingly) I threw the maid out the door—

Bernie (trying to stop her)

Bong! Bong! Bong!

Marsha

Yesterday, I put the remains of the sauce in the buffet. Fine. What do I see? She put turkey stuffing with the potato salad. Can you imagine? I said: "Bessie—"

Bernie

No—

Marsha

I said: "Bessie, don't pretend you didn't do it. You put the stuffing with the potato salad!" Well, can you believe—she tried to deny it. She said: "Oh no, Ma'am, I did not." Can you believe that? So I said: "Bessie—"

Bernie

Enough!

Marsha

"Bessie, don't lie to me," and she said:—

Bernie

Stop, Jezebel! This story is upsetting me. My jaw is stiff! My hair is standing on end. I want you to go. Go away, Marsha, go away. (Marsha looks right at him and begins to remove her coat with extraordinary tranquility) DON'T YOU DARE TAKE OFF YOUR COAT!

Marsha

I do so dare!

Bernie (wildly)

You've been here too long. Too long! They're going to make you go any minute.

Marsha

Bernie, are you lucid?

Bernie

Clear as a bell.

Marsha (doubtfully)

Are you positive?

Bernie

Lucid. Transparent. You can see my clapper.

Marsha

Stay that way. I've got a surprise for you.

Bernie

No surprises. Surprises give me a pain.

Marsha (embracing him)

Hold me!

Bernie (giving her a quick hug)

There! Bye, bye.

Marsha

No bye-bye.

Bernie

Sorry you have to go.

Marsha

No, I don't.

Bernie

Huh?

Marsha

Great news, sweetheart, we're never going to part again.

Bernie

Nonsense.

Marsha

Let me explain.

Bernie

Bong. I understand without your telling me. Bong. You see me like this, and then—and then suddenly I have this evil fantasy. I want to decapitate a woman while running around naked. (starting to remove his shirt)

Marsha

You're cute naked—

Bernie (pulling a set of official papers out of a drawer)

Read these rules. Two visits per week. Thirty minutes per visit. Doctor's orders. The Doctor will get mad. See you next week, baby.

Marsha

Are you going to let me explain?

Bernie

No.

Marsha

I said before that we're never going to part again.

Bernie

I don't want to come home.

Marsha

Who said anything about your coming home, silly? I'm coming to stay with you.

Bernie (smugly, quite confident it's impossible)

You can't. It's against the rules.

Marsha

Rules! Shit!

Bernie

Shit yourself. They won't let you. So there!

Marsha

We'll see about that.

Bernie

Madame, this is not an hotel.

Marsha

Queen Jezebel to you.

Bernie

Begone from Israel, O Harlot Queen, lest evil befall you. Get out. Begone! Begone!

(Marsha calmly rings for an orderly.)

Bernie (instantly aware of danger)

Why are you calling for an orderly?

Marsha

I want to see the Doctor. You see, one night I couldn't sleep. I was mad at you. I had an idea. (pulls a flashlight out of her bag)

Bernie (nervously)

What's that?

Marsha

A torch.

Bernie

What is all this?

Marsha

You'll see soon enough. There's an empty room across the hall. I'm going to take it.

Bernie

You? No!

Marsha

Me! Yes! And then we can be together again. I'm not worldly. I've seen enough plays, been to enough social events. I don't even like television. So, I'm going to retire—with you!

Bernie

Now, wait a minute.

Marsha

It will be like a second honeymoon.

Bernie

Now, you just stop right now.

Marsha

Only it will be better than a second honeymoon. It will never end.

Bernie

It's against the law. It's strictly forbidden. It's bad for my mental state. Out Jezebel!

Marsha

No more maids to put stuffing in the potato salad. It will be like a dream.

Bernie

A dream!

Marsha

Shh! Not another word. Here comes the Doctor. Now, watch and see how smart your little wifey is.

(Enter Dr. Watson.)

Watson

Is something wrong?

Marsha (in a strange voice)

Where am I?

Watson

Excuse me?

Marsha

Where am I?

Bernie

Pay no attention, Doctor. It's a joke. A sick joke.

Watson (professionally)

Wait, please. Let her speak.

Marsha (brandishing her flashlight, which she has now turned on)

Give me your poor, your wretched—

Bernie (anxiously)

Don't listen to her, Doc. She's doing this to annoy me.

Marsha.

I'm the Lady? Right, Doctor?

Bernie (scornfully)

You'd have to be a pretty stupid doctor to be fooled by a childish prank like this. (then, frightened, he realizes the doctor would have to be pretty stupid to be taken in by his ploy) That is to say—

Marsha

The husband is the Liberty Bell, and the wife is the Statue of Liberty.

Watson

Very likely. Who else would marry a bell? Who but a bell would marry a statue?

Bernie (helplessly)

He's a flaming idiot!

Marsha

I brandish my torch. Where is my room?

Watson

I'll arrange everything. You just wait.

Marsha

I am forever. I am eternal.

Watson

Be right back. Don't go anywhere. What an interesting case. Dr. Freud never had anything like this.

(Exit Dr. Watson.)

Marsha (putting out her flashlight)

You see how easy it is!

Bernie

Shame on you! To make a fool of the good doctor.

Marsha (innocently)

Have I done anything wrong? I ask myself why I didn't do it sooner? I was wasting away without you.

(hugging him) We'll be as snug as two bugs in a rug! From time to time I'll be Miss Liberty.

Bernie

But think of the expense!

Marsha

Bah! The insurance will pay.

Bernie

Besides, men are kept apart from the women patients.

Marsha

They'll make an exception for a married couple.

Bernie (in agony)

No.

Marsha (joyfully)

Yes! This place needs a little cleaning. You're such a slob, Bernie.

(Marsha starts rearranging things, much to Bernie's horror.)

Bernie

What are you doing?

Marsha (moving his easel)

Cleaning up a little.

Bernie

Don't you touch my stuff!

Marsha

Phew! It smells bad in here. You were smoking with that bastard Lattimore.

Bernie

So what?

Marsha

Give me that damn pipe.

Bernie

Don't you touch me. I'm a bell.

Marsha

I don't give a damn.

Bernie

Bong!

Marsha

That was okay when I was only staying for a half hour. But not any more. The next time you become a bell, I'm going to smack you.

Bernie

I'm a parchment. I'm flaking. I'm dry. I'm combustible.

Marsha

And I'm going to kick you twice when you're a parchment.

(Reenter Dr. Watson.)

Watson

The room is ready. This way, please, Miss Liberty.

Marsha (pulling out her flashlight again and snapping it on)

I'm coming. I bring you light. Give me your poor. (to Bernie) After lights out, I'll sneak in. (whispering romantically) We'll sleep in the same bed.

(Marsha and Dr. Watson exit. Bernie runs and grabs Dr. Watson by his coattails.)

Bernie

Watson, a word, I beg.

Watson

What is it?

Bernie

Close the door.

Watson (humoring him)

All right. (closing the door) Now what?

Bernie (after some thought)

My wife is an impostor.

Watson

Really?

Bernie (significantly)

An impostor.

Watson

You're certain, my dear colleague?

Bernie

Very. She just now confessed that she's crazy to be with me.

Watson

She wouldn't be crazy except to be with you?

Bernie

Exactly.

Watson (somewhat peeved)

I didn't think you were so conceited.

Bernie

You don't understand. She's always trying to annoy me.

Watson

We'll look into that.

Bernie

You're not listening to me because you think I'm crazy. Well, it's time to enlighten you: I AM NOT CRAZY!

Watson

Ha, ha.

Bernie

I only pretended to be crazy.

Watson

Why do that?

Bernie

So as to get away from my wife. But now that she's planning to reside here, it's time to confess the truth.

Watson

So, as I understand it, you pretended insanity to get away from your wife?

Bernie (folding his arms triumphantly)

A precise diagnosis.

Watson

And your wife, being lonely, is pretending to be crazy so she can be with you?

Bernie

Exactly.

Watson

Then, neither one of you is crazy? Is that case, I'm going to release you both.

Bernie

Now, wait a minute! You can't do that.

Watson

Why not? It's simple enough.

Bernie

Listen—I believe I'm a bell again. I'm going to ring immediately. RING!

Watson

Very interesting, but I'm in a hurry—

Bernie

My wife, however, is very healthy. Very healthy.

Watson

At first glance. But I cannot deny I always thought she was a little—not playing with a full deck, if you know what I mean.

Bernie

Her story doesn't hold water.

Watson

Does the business about being a bell or a parchment? Take a little advice, my friend—

Bernie

What is it?

Watson

Take a nap. You'll feel better later. Right now, you bore me.

(Enter Marsha, somewhat disheveled, with a broom and mop.)

Marsha

Bernie, help me sweep up.

Bernie

It's starting again.

Marsha

What kind of cleaning staff do you have here, Doctor?

Bernie

You see, Doctor?

Marsha (seeing the Doctor and snapping on her flashlight)

Give me your poor—

Bernie

Don't listen, Doc. She's crazy, like me.

Watson

Exactly what I've been thinking.

Marsha

Give me your poor— (totally normal) Bernie, I want some help with the dusting.

Bernie

Go home, Marsha. You'll keep it up until I scalp you.

Watson

Come on. (getting between them) That's enough.

Marsha

Here I am, carrying the torch, and the bastard wants to attack me.

Bernie

Put it out. People have seen enough.

Marsha

Who's boss here?

Bernie

I am.

Marsha (folding her arms)

Miss Liberty doesn't take orders from a Dumb Bell!

Bernie (also folding his arms)

Or a Liberty Bell from a dumb statue.

Marsha (kicking him)

Or a man who thinks he's a parchment.

Bernie

Bong. RING! BONG! RING!

Marsha (stamping her foot)

Give me your poor!

Watson (shaking his head)

An extremely contagious disease transmitted by marital consanguinity. I'll call it—Bernard's Complaint!

(Enter Henry the VIII)

Henry

What a lot of noise. (stares at Marsha) It can't be! It's Anne Boleyn! (rushes to her) Can you forgive me, Nan? I loved you best of all my wives.

(Bernie shouts "Bong!" Marsha hits Henry the VIII on the head with her flashlight.)

Watson

Poor Dr. Freud. He never had a case like this.

CURTAIN FALLS AMID BEDLAM

THE WRITING LESSON
SUGGESTED BY A STORY BY ILYA ILF AND YEVGENI PETROV

CAST OF CHARACTERS

The Writer

The Editor

THE PLAY

The editor's office. Moscow in the 1930s.

The offices of the magazine Adventure. *It is small, shabby, and decorated only with a large, smiling portrait of Chairman Stalin at his most beneficent. There is a samovar. The window looks out on the Kremlin. Everything is cozy, the editor is a most pompous person, easily agitated and probably not very competent. He is looking over some manuscripts which he throws down in disgust.*

Editor

Nobody can write these days, but every scribbler in Moscow is writing. And I have to read it!

(There is a timid knock at the door.)

Come in, come in.

(The writer enters. He is a man in his twenties, intellectual and timid.)

Writer

Excuse me, Comrade Editor. I—

Editor

Well, what do you want? I'm sorry, but I rejected your novel. Perhaps with work, but—

Writer

But I—

Editor

What do you want from me? I can't publish something like that. And I—I don't give writing lessons.

Writer

But—

Editor

But what? Can't you see I'm busy. Get out!

Writer

But, you sent for me.

Editor

Forgive me, Constantine Demitrovich, forgive me. I thought it was one of those scribblers who constantly keep sending me manuscripts. I have never had the pleasure of meeting you before. Please, please. A distinguished writer such as yourself, you must never think— Sit down, sit down. Will you have tea or vodka?

Writer

Vodka, if you don't mind.

Editor

Champagne for you, Constantine Demitrovich—if I could get any. But, vodka it is. (pours drinks) Skol! (they both swill down their drinks) Another? (pours more drinks) Skol!

Writer

Good vodka. But, if I may ask—?

Editor

Of course, of course, to business, eh? Comrade writer, you must understand that we have simply run out of fresh interesting material to print in our magazine.

Writer

Comrade editor, I—

Editor

Exactly, Comrade writer, exactly. Adventure magazine is the leading publication for Soviet youth. We maintain the highest standards here. But the trash we've been receiving lately— So, we call on you.

Writer

Comrade editor—

Editor

You're perfectly right. Our literature is too didactic. We need something—

Writer

Original.

Editor

Gripping.

Writer

From the life of the people.

Editor

In short, a Soviet Robinson Crusoe.

Writer

Robinson Crusoe?

Editor

Comrade writer, you have a bad habit of repeating everything I say, not to mention interrupting.

Writer

Comrade editor—

Editor

Do you think you can manage it?

Writer

I—

Editor

Of course you can do it. You are a Stalin Prize winner.

Writer

I—

Editor

Don't pretend you're suffering from writer's cramp. When the Party calls, you must respond.

Writer

I—

Editor

Please stop interrupting.

Writer

(furious)

I CAN DO IT!

Editor

Well, why didn't you say so, Comrade? You beat around the bush so much. This may be the most difficult, significant book that you have ever written.

Writer

It seems to me that plagiarizing Robinson Crusoe ought to be easy.

Editor

But not just any Robinson Crusoe.

Writer

Robinson Crusoe is Robinson Crusoe.

Editor

It must be a Soviet Robinson Crusoe.

Writer

All right, all right. What do you expect, a Romanian Robinson Crusoe?

Editor

Ha, ah. A Romanian Robinson Crusoe! I'll drink to that. Skol! You writers must have your little jokes.

Writer

Here it is. A Soviet youth is shipwrecked. A wave washes him ashore on a desert island. He finds himself alone, defenseless—face to face with the hostile powers of nature.

Editor

I like it. I like it.

Writer

He is beset with dangers, wild animals, snakes, the monsoon.

Editor

Good, good.

Writer

But the Soviet Robinson Crusoe overcomes every insuperable obstacle.

Editor

(excitedly)

From studying the thoughts of Comrade Stalin and the teachings of the Party.

Writer

(gulping)

Right, right, Comrade editor. Three years later, he is found by a Soviet expedition, bursting with life and health. He has built himself a hut, bred rabbits, and taught a parrot to wake him up with the words: "Attention, attention! Off with your blanket, time for early morning exercises."

Editor

This is great stuff. No wonder you won the Stalin Prize. That bit about the rabbits is a stroke of genius. But, you know, I'm not quite clear about your theme.

Writer

Man's struggle with nature.

Editor

That's true, of course, but I don't see anything particularly Soviet about that.

Writer

(desperately)

What about the parrot? He takes the place of radio propaganda broadcasts. Radio Moscow, so to speak.

Editor

The parrot is brilliant. Brilliant. But, where is the sense of Soviet Community Life?

Writer

(incredulously)

On an uninhabited island?

Editor

And the local trade union committee?

Writer

What?

Editor

The guiding light of the trade unions is the heart of Soviet policy! I have no literary pretensions myself, but in your place, Comrade writer, I would insinuate the idea of a local trade union committee.

Writer

Insinuate—insinuate, but the whole idea of the book is based on the idea of isolation.

Editor

Don't be so literal. There's got to be a way to do it. We are paying you for your ingenuity and imagination.

Writer

All right, all right. Why didn't I see that before? There must be two survivors of the shipwreck. Robinson Crusoe and the president of the local trade union committee.

Editor

And two full-time trade union workers.

Writer

Help!

Editor

And one female activist in charge of collecting membership dues.

Writer

How can she collect membership dues when they don't have any money?

Editor

Maybe they use wampum or something. Anyway, she can collect Robinson Crusoe's dues.

Writer

The president can collect Robinson Crusoe's dues.

Editor

That's where you're wrong, Comrade writer. The president can't be allowed to occupy himself with such trifles. He must devote himself to serious work, guiding and leading.

Writer

Well, better have her, then. Maybe it's not a bad idea. A little love interest. She can marry Robinson Crusoe or the president. That's it! They fight over her.

Editor

Absolutely not! Adventure is a wholesome magazine designed for young readers. No cheap bourgeois romance or unhealthy eroticism. Just let her collect membership dues and keep them in her safe.

Writer

Please, Comrade editor, there cannot be a safe on an uninhabited island.

Editor

Why not?

Writer

Why not?

Editor

Why not?

Writer

(livid)

Because it's ridiculous, that's why not.

Editor

(icily)

A safe is absolutely essential.

Writer

For God's sake, why?

Editor

(as to a child)

So no one will steal the membership dues.

Writer

But, who will steal the funds?

Editor

What about Robinson Crusoe, the president of the committee, the two workers, or the saboteurs?

Writer

(dangerously)

The saboteurs?

Editor

(complacently)

Certainly. The anti-party faction. The wreckers. The Kulaks. The remnants of the old aristocracy.

Writer

But—

Editor

I don't want to inhibit your creativity. These are just suggestions—

Writer

Of course.

Editor

The Party encourages the highest standards of literary merit. But, the first thing, lad, is to depict the masses. The broad stratum of Soviet workers. You can't leave that out.

Writer

BUT THE ISLAND IS UNINHABITED!

Editor

Why does it have to be uninhabited? Don't confuse everything. There's this big island—or better yet, a subcontinent—and on it there takes place this series of gripping and original adventures. Right from Robinson Crusoe, of course. The trade union is not well organized, and the female activist discovers a series of discrepancies. The president is stealing the dues. And the broad masses come to her aid. There's your story, young man!

Writer

What about Robinson Crusoe?

Editor

Get rid of him. He's ruining the whole story.

Writer

But—

Editor

And that shipwreck is quite unnecessary. Let's do it without the shipwreck.

Writer

Can we have a murder?

Editor

A murder?

Writer

Yes.

Editor

Whose?

Writer

(pouncing on him and choking him to death gleefully)

Yours! It will add suspense. You see, the saboteur, or make that the Kulak, murders the president of the local committee. How's that for a surprise ending?

(The writer releases the limp body of the editor. He picks up his hat and goes towards the door. Suddenly the editor sits up and whistles.)

Editor

Great, great, Comrade! But, realism, realism. Socialist realism.

This is petty bourgeois fantasy and romanticism. No, no. In real life, in Soviet life, the NKVD comes and arrests the writer for bourgeois deviationism.

(Stalin smiles as the curtain falls.)

CURTAIN

ABOUT THE AUTHOR

Frank J. Morlock has written and translated many plays since retiring from the legal profession in 1992. His translations have also appeared on Project Gutenberg, the Alexandre Dumas Père web page, Literature in the Age of Napoléon, Infinite Artistries.com, and Munsey's (formerly Blackmask). In 2006 he received an award from the North American Jules Verne Society for his translations of Verne's plays. He lives and works in México.

www.ingramcontent.com/pod-product-compliance
Lightning Source LLC
LaVergne TN
LVHW041615070426
835507LV00008B/243

www.ingramcontent.com/pod-product-compliance
Lightning Source LLC
LaVergne TN
LVHW041614070426
835507LV00008B/233